T0405575

GIRL GENIUS

Bold breakthroughs from women in science

By CARLA SINCLAIR

Illustrated by GEORGIA RUCKER

downtown bookworks

Downtown Bookworks Inc.
265 Canal Street, New York, NY 10013
www.downtownbookworks.com

Copyright © 2019 Downtown Bookworks Inc.
Designed and illustrated by Georgia Rucker
Printed in China, December 2019
10 9 8 7 6 5 4 3 2 1

CONTENTS

FOREWORD

The book you're holding has the wrong name. The girls, ladies, and women in this book are not geniuses!

When we think of geniuses, sure, we think of folks with high IQs who have some preternatural—or out-of-this-world—talent. But most of these people were not born with superhuman abilities—no huge pulsating brains or inventing calculus at age seven. Instead, they're everyday humans who care so much that they've fully unlocked their totally normal brain's potential. That's why you aren't going to see any stats like their ACT/SAT scores or how they did in math class.

You are a human, just like everyone in this book . . . and humans are amazing! We can find patterns, absorb research, learn from history, make connections between different disciplines of science and the humanities, and communicate with other humans. All of these skills are essential to creating, discovering, and preserving the world around us—more so than whether you have memorized the elements of the periodic table.

As you flip through this book, reading about different experiments and adventures that have led to discoveries, I'd like you to think about how each person used a variety of skills and interests together to chart her own path. The scientists and inventors in the book may have a main passion. But whether it's fashion, medicine, music, robotics, animal care, space travel, or biology, that core interest was combined with two other powerful forces. The first is a desire to share discovery—to explore the world and universe we live in, heal and care for the sick, make people laugh, push the human body to create new sounds and movement, or ease the pain and suffering in the world. And all of these are valid and worthy interests! The second is the unrelenting practice and patience of working through the failures, the drudgery, and the disappointment of trying different things until, at long last, there is glorious success.

The genius documented in these pages is how each woman took those three elements—the head (how they think and learn and study), the heart (how they are focused on and work with others), and the hands (how they practice, document, and create). This triangle of support is what leads to each creation, invention, and discovery—and it's what will lead you to do the same!

When I said the women in this book weren't geniuses, I forgot to tell you something else: the "girl" in the title of this book isn't in the book either. She's the one holding this book. And, once you've read it, I want you to think about how to combine your head, your heart, and your hands to perfect your art and share it with the rest of us.

—LIMOR FRIED

Maker, artist, engineer, and
founder and CEO of Adafruit Industries

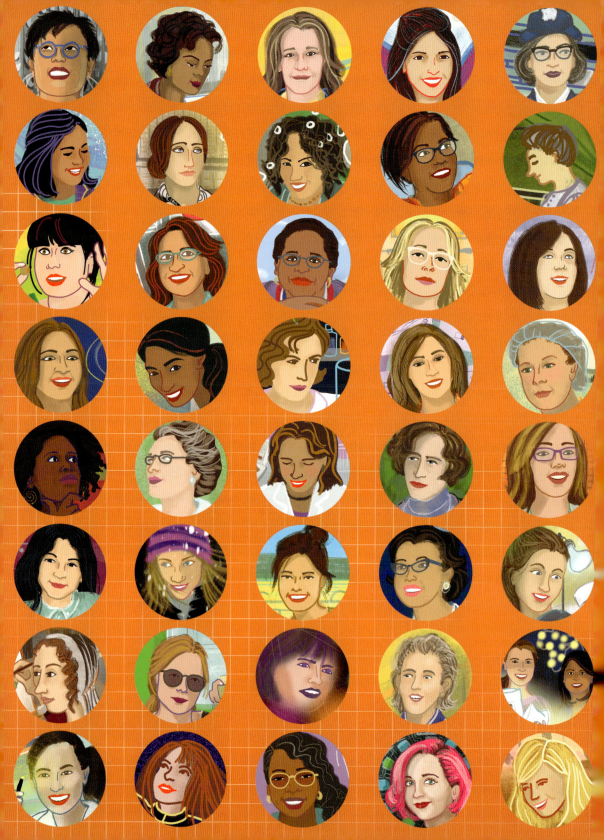

INTRODUCTION

Have you ever made a potion out of liquids and goop found in your kitchen? Planted seeds and watched them grow? Mixed different paints together to see what color you'd get? Spent your day observing how animals behave? Figured out a solution to an annoying problem? Imagined ways to make the world a better place? If you answered yes to any of these questions, this book is for you!

With curiosity and imagination, the 40 girls and women in these pages have dreamed up "what ifs," tackled scientific conundrums, and experimented with materials and ideas. As a new college student in Massachusetts, Star Simpson invented a delivery drone called TacoCopter after asking herself, "What if a drone could bring me a taco?" In Mexico, professor Sandra Pascoe Ortiz turned cactus slime into plastic after wondering, "What if people could make planet-friendly plastic?" When Keiana Cavé was 18 years old, she created a molecule that cleans the ocean after imagining, "What if there was something that could eat up the toxins polluting the Gulf of Mexico after an oil spill?" And physicist Lene Hau shocked the scientific community when her experiments answered the question, "What if I shine the fastest thing on Earth (light) through the coldest thing in the world?" (Spoiler alert: she literally stopped light.)

These inventions and all the other amazing discoveries and creations made by the women in this book might sound too incredible for the average person to do, but they're not! All it takes to start is the ability to marvel at the world, to question how things work, to imagine something new or better than what already exists, and then to ask "What if?" That simple question, along with research, experiments, and confidence that you can make it happen, can turn a wild idea into an extraordinary reality.

The women in this book are just like the rest of us. They come from all over the world, from different kinds of families, and each has her own stories to tell. For instance, before veterinary surgeon Michelle Oblak saved a dog's life by removing a humongous tumor from the pup's head and then 3-D printing her a new skull, she was a kid from Canada who always wanted to work with animals. When chemist Mandë Holford was growing up in New York City, she was always interested in science and went to the American Museum of Natural History "all the time." Now she travels around the planet to find killer snails so she can turn their deadly venom into lifesaving medicine. Computer engineer Chieko Asakawa from Japan was an athletic girl until an accident at age 11 left her blind. Now she invents smartphone apps and robots that help blind people get around in public places. Food scientist Maria Andrade, from the small island country of Cape Verde, always dreamed of doing something big. Now she breeds special vitamin-packed sweet potatoes to help fight malnutrition in Africa.

Some of the women in this book, like Rachel Zimmerman Brachman and Allie Weber, were teenagers when they made their scientific discoveries and inventions, while others, like Helen B. Taussig and Temple Grandin, had been working in their fields for decades. Many of the women, like roboticist Carol Reiley and product designer Sha Yao, keep coming up with clever solutions to today's problems, while others, like insect expert Maria Sibylla Merian and Nobel Prize–winning physicist Marie Curie, lived in previous centuries.

Some, like 14-year-old inventor Gitanjali Rao, were encouraged to follow their interests in science and math by their teachers or parents, while others, like Katherine Johnson, who calculated spaceflights for NASA, faced discrimination for their gender, disability, or race. Some grew up in big cities, like YouTube's popular robot inventor Simone Giertz from Stockholm, Sweden. Others, like moldable-glue inventor Jane ní Dhulchaointigh from Kilkenny, Ireland, were raised in small towns. While everyone in this book is her own unique person, as innovators they all started off with the same simple thing: an idea.

Along with having ideas, they also share other similarities. For instance, a lot of these women admit to being very curious as children. Fiona Wood, an Australian who invented spray-on skin for people who have survived severe burns, once said she was a *why* kind of kid, as in "Why is it working? Why does it do that? Why, why, why, why?" And Ayah Bdeir, who created the popular electronics kit littleBits, was so curious, she pulled her sisters' toys apart to see what was inside (they weren't too happy about that!). As a child, Navy computer coder Grace Hopper had the habit of taking all the clocks apart in her house just to see how they worked (much to her mother's chagrin!).

Many of these women invented cool things, but some, like planetary geologist Adriana Ocampo, who helped solve the mystery of dinosaur extinction by looking at the world from space, and plant biologist Monica Gagliano, who devises experiments to test whether plants are capable of remembering things, are busy uncovering new information about the planet and the things that grow and thrive on it.

One of the most important similarities these women have—one that has made each of them successful—is the way they think about mistakes. Rather than quitting after a failed experiment, they welcome mistakes. They know that mistakes teach scientists and inventors what doesn't work, and what not to do. From there, scientists can try new ways of doing something until they find the right solution. As 19-year-old Hannah Herbst, who invented a device that turns ocean water into electricity, once said, "Be quirky, excited, confident, and embrace failure!"

Until recently, STEM (science, technology, engineering, and math) was like a boys' club that tried to keep girls out. But because of trailblazers like the innovative women in this book, things are starting to change. Girls who grow up to make robots, develop new lifesaving medicines, fly into outer space, discover new species of animals, and invent amazing things are girls who never let other people's discouraging words get in their way. They might sometimes get frustrated, but they never give up. They pursue STEM because they love exploring, experimenting, building with Legos or electronics, observing nature, looking through a microscope, and asking the question, "What if?"

If you also love to let your genius shine and want to make a difference—either for yourself, for your community, or for the world— you don't have to wait. As 14-year-old inventor and YouTuber Allie Weber says, "Kids are not the future, we are here now. We are not going to change the world someday, we are already doing it."

—CARLA SINCLAIR

Helen B. Taussig

INVESTIGATE **NEW THEORIES** TO KEEP BABIES SAFE

Helen B. Taussig, born in 1898 in Cambridge, Massachusetts, had her share of hardship. When she was 11 years old, her mother died from tuberculosis (TB), a disease that attacks the lungs. Taussig then contracted TB, which affected her health as a child. She also struggled with dyslexia, a reading disability that wasn't understood well in the early 1900s. As if these challenges weren't enough, she also became deaf in her thirties. But her struggles didn't stop her from inventing a way to save thousands of babies' lives. In fact, they made her stronger.

Becoming a doctor wasn't easy for a woman in the early part of the 20th century. Even Taussig's father told her that medicine wasn't a good degree for women. He suggested that perhaps studying public health would be better. Then a dean at Harvard University told her that although she could take classes in their public health program, Harvard would never give her a degree because she was a woman. Of course, her meeting with the dean was a disappointment. But rather than quitting, she let his discouraging words embolden her. And she decided that she would study medicine, with or without her father's approval, and that she would find a school that offered degrees to women. In 1927, she earned her medical degree from Johns Hopkins University School of Medicine.

"WHAT SEEMED TO BE DISAPPOINTMENT . . . LATER PROVED TO BE A GREAT OPPORTUNITY."

Taussig worked in *cardiology* (an area of medicine that specializes in the heart) at Johns Hopkins Hospital, one of the best hospitals in the country. She was so bright that the hospital soon made her head of the *pediatric cardiac clinic* (the children's ward for heart patients). Around this time (when she was 32), Taussig had a devastating setback. She lost her hearing due to a childhood case of whooping cough. Being deaf makes it impossible to listen to heartbeats. So she developed a method of "listening" to someone's heart with her fingertips. She thought it worked even better than using a stethoscope! She learned to use a new device called a fluoroscope, which showed X-rays of the heart, arteries, and lungs on a screen, and she began to carefully learn everything she could from the images of hearts.

Taussig was particularly interested in *cyanotic* babies, or "blue babies." These infants have a rare heart disorder that causes them to look blue. At the time, doctors wrongly believed these babies had suffered a heart attack, for which there was no treatment. Most of these babies died, and those who survived ended up in wheelchairs. But Taussig suspected something else was causing the syndrome. By expertly using her fingertip method to examine heartbeats and patiently observing defective hearts using the fluoroscope, she noticed something other doctors had missed. Babies are born with an extra opening in their hearts called the ductus arteriosus. This opening closes a couple of days after birth. But when the ductus closes up in blue babies, their symptoms worsen because they are left with one less opening for the blood to circulate through.

This validated Taussig's theory that heart attacks don't cause blue baby syndrome, but instead that it is caused by low circulation due to a lack of oxygen in the blood. "I immediately thought, 'Well, if you could close a ductus, why can't you *build* a ductus?' That would help these children and keep them alive," she later said. And even though she thought it was possible, she later admitted, "I didn't realize *how much* it would help them."

Taussig told her idea to Dr. Robert Gross, a specialist in the field, who said it might be possible, but he wasn't interested in pursuing the idea. Building a ductus and then inserting it into a baby seemed too problematic. But Taussig did not give up. Three years later, she challenged another surgeon, Dr. Alfred Blalock, who had just performed surgery. "Dr. Blalock, you've done a very nice job closing this ductus; why can't you build a ductus?" she asked. "To some of our cyanotic children, it would mean a life for them." He liked the idea. In 1944, Taussig, Blalock, and Blalock's assistant, skilled technician Vivien Thomas, built a ductus-like tube, or shunt, and perfected a technique that led to a treatment that has saved tens of thousands of babies' lives and is still used today.

But Taussig wasn't through saving babies' lives. A decade later, a horrifying outbreak occurred in Europe—thousands of babies were being born with shortened, malformed arms and legs. Nobody knew what was causing it. Some doctors began to suspect *thalidomide*, a new anti-anxiety drug doctors prescribed to pregnant women around the world to help with nausea. So Taussig flew to Germany, researched the epidemic, and concluded that thalidomide caused birth defects. She publicized her findings, testified in front of Congress to ban the drug, helped put a stop to its distribution, and changed how the FDA (Food and Drug Administration) evaluates drugs.

In 1964, President Lyndon Johnson awarded Taussig the Presidential Medal of Freedom, saying, "Her fundamental concepts have made possible the modern surgery of the heart, which enables countless children to lead productive lives."

Gitanjali Rao

RESEARCH, RESEARCH, RESEARCH—AND **REACH OUT** TO EXPERTS

Gitanjali Rao is your typical teenager in many ways. She plays the piano, spends a lot of time baking, and takes fencing lessons, which she loves. She also enjoys chemistry experiments—especially when things blow up or change colors. But Gitanjali has also done something that makes her stand out from everyone else: she has invented a device that can detect poisonous lead in water.

When Gitanjali was around nine years old, she was eating dinner when she saw something horrifying on TV. It was a news segment about how the drinking water in Flint, Michigan, is polluted with lead. For years, Flint's toxic water has made many people, especially children, very sick, but no one has fixed the problem. "It was so difficult for me to accept that there were kids who were drinking poison while I'm over here drinking clean water," said Gitanjali, from her home in the outskirts of Denver, Colorado.

The story about contaminated water upset her so much that she couldn't stop thinking about it. She persuaded her parents to check the lead in their own water. She discovered that the only home tests available were flimsy strips that you dip in water. Gitanjali explained that using them took "quite a few tries" because the strips were "not reliable at all." (The water in her home turned out to be fine.) But it bothered her that the available kits for testing water at home weren't dependable. What if the people in Flint—or anywhere else in the world—used one of these tests and got the wrong result? They might drink tainted water without realizing it was harmful!

This experience got her thinking. What if she could invent a small device that would quickly and accurately measure the level of lead in water, and then immediately send the results via Bluetooth to an app on your phone?

Like most kids, Gitanjali didn't know that much about the science behind lead-contaminated water. So she did what all scientists do: she followed the story in the news and researched the problem—not for days, not for weeks, but for a couple of years! She even visited Flint, where she drank only bottled water for two days. "It's really scary," she says, "to see a place in America that is so lacking in clean water to drink."

As she came up with ideas about how to build her water tester, she taught herself to code. She also asked a lot of questions. "I had to reach out to a lot of experts in the field to talk about my device and see what improvements I could make." By the time she was 11, she had a cardboard *prototype* (an early example of a product before it has been perfected) of her device. She called the device Tethys, after the Greek goddess of fresh water.

Gitanjali entered Tethys in the 2017 Discovery Education 3M Young Scientist Challenge, a contest for middle school students with great ideas. And she became a finalist! Then 3M invited all of

"WE CAN COLLECTIVELY SOLVE PROBLEMS IN SOCIETY AND ENCOURAGE SCIENCE AND TECHNOLOGY."

the finalists to spend the summer at their lab, each working with a 3M scientist to improve their prototype. Gitanjali was so excited to work at the 3M lab that she "screamed her head off" when she got home. She would get to wear a white lab coat and goggles while she coded the software, 3-D printed the hardware in plastic, worked on the chemistry, and improved her design for Tethys.

She worked hard and used her new resources well. After that summer, she and the other finalists presented their upgraded prototypes to the judges. Gitanjali, now a seventh grader, won the challenge, and 3M awarded her a $25,000 prize! She used her winnings to further her research and improve her invention.

Since then, she has partnered with an environmental organization called Pace Analytical that is helping her make easily reproducible versions of Tethys and test it in the real world. "I'm looking at creating 50 reproducible devices to do real field testing, starting with places like Flint and schools around other water sources," she says. She wants Tethys, which fits in the palm of your hand, to become "a standard testing tool that anybody can use."

Inventing something that changes lives for the better is challenging and time-consuming, but Gitanjali, who hopes to go to the Massachusetts Institute of Technology (MIT) after high school, never gave up. While working on Tethys, she says there was a lot of trying and failing in order to discover what really worked. The whole process taught her a lot. Gitanjali has some great advice for other teenagers and future inventors: "Don't be afraid to try. That's what held me back when I first started inventing." She says, "I was scared that I was going to fail. But then you realize that failure is just another step to success."

Maria Sibylla Merian

BE PATIENT—AND
RECORD THE DETAILS

Maria Sibylla Merian, born in Germany in 1647, was not afraid of insects. In fact, they were all she ever thought about. She loved watching how they ate and moved, and she would spend days or even weeks watching just one insect. Her patience and fascination with these creatures led her to become one of the world's first *entomologists*, or insect experts.

Merian's obsession with insects began with silkworms when she was 13 years old. She was constantly outdoors with a paintbrush in hand, using watercolors (at the time, women weren't supposed to use other types of paints!) to illustrate every detail she noticed about silkworms. She started bringing silkworms into her house and keeping them in containers with mulberry leaves for food. That way, she could watch a silkworm for hours as it chomped on leaves, spun a "date pit" (cocoon), or emerged from the cocoon as a moth. She painted beautiful, accurate pictures of what she saw. While the world still believed in *spontaneous generation*, the mistaken idea that insects, such as maggots, sprouted from nonliving things, like rotting meat, she was documenting how a silkworm's life cycle really worked.

Merian's enthusiasm for silkworms expanded to moths and butterflies, and after getting married at age 18, she crammed her kitchen (which became her lab) with jars, boxes, plants, and an army of caterpillars. She would stay awake all night studying a caterpillar's movement or waiting for a butterfly to break out of its chrysalis so she could draw it. This left her little time for friends. "I withdrew from society and devoted myself to these investigations," she said.

Right after her second daughter was born, she wrote *The Wondrous Transformation of Caterpillars,* the first science book of its kind. While other scientists drew insects that were alone against plain backgrounds, Merian drew them realistically. She showed a party of busy caterpillars on a tall flowery plant, crawling, exploring, and munching on leaves filled with holes. Another illustration showed a green spiky caterpillar sharing a hanging, overripe grapefruit with a brown moth. These vivid, lifelike illustrations helped readers get a better sense of how the creatures lived.

Maybe because of her time-consuming work as a *naturalist* (a person who studies creatures in their natural habitat), her marriage fell apart. She and her daughters moved to Amsterdam, a city in the Netherlands, where women could live independently. In this bustling city, Merian was able to support herself and her daughters by selling her illustrations to scientists and art collectors. But even more thrilling than making money from her work was getting to see insects from other countries. At the time, the Netherlands was a hub for traders from around the world, so Merian met importers who showed her exotic insects from the East and West Indies and from South America.

Although it was truly exciting for Merian to see these exotic insects, they were dead. And Merian, who spent so much time studying insect movement and behavior, wanted to see them alive, in their natural habitat! So at age 52, she made a daring decision. She boarded a ship with her younger daughter and traveled for two months across the ocean to live in Surinam, a small Dutch colony off the coast of South America. (It is now an independent country called

Suriname.) It was highly uncommon in those days for a woman to be a naturalist, to travel without a man, and to travel for the sole reason of scientific exploration. But nothing Merian did was common. She chopped her way through jungles, took small boats on rivers through the lush rain forest, and climbed up trees in order to collect insects unfamiliar to Europeans. Within two years, she came down with an illness, probably malaria, which feels like the flu and can be deadly if not treated. She went back to Amsterdam to heal, bringing her drawings and preserved insects with her.

In South America, Merian had seen things in nature that Europeans knew nothing about: tropical lizards, tarantulas that attacked birds, and aggressive ants that quickly sawed their way through leaves, just to name a few. She illustrated and wrote about them all in her stunning masterpiece, *Insects of Surinam*, published in 1705. The book was considered to be dramatic and even frightening. One painting in the book was of a huge hairy tarantula sitting on top of an upside-down hummingbird, with the description: "They take small birds from their nests and suck all the blood from their bodies."

The book was a sensation, and Merian became famous across Europe. Even King George III bought her illustrations, which are still kept at Buckingham Palace in London! Unfortunately, about a century later, during the Victorian age, people stopped recognizing women as scientists and artists. Merian's work was teased and criticized. People said it was impossible for tarantulas to eat birds. They were wrong, but her work and fame disappeared and only recently reemerged.

Today Merian is recognized as a brilliant naturalist who described more than 200 types of insects throughout her career. She is remembered as the pioneer that she was: a respected—and very patient—entomologist.

The Wondrous Transformation of Caterpillars

Maria Sibylla Merian

Carol Reiley

NEVER UNDERESTIMATE
WHAT ROBOTS CAN DO

Ever since Carol Reiley was young, she's wanted to save lives. As a teenager living in Washington State, she volunteered at a hospital, which is where she first learned what a *pacemaker* was. It's a device that helps a person's heart beat properly. A light bulb switched on in her head: She didn't want to be a doctor who helps one person at a time. Instead, she wanted to invent things that could help millions of lives at once.

And for nearly 20 years, she's done just that. Robotics is her specialty. From developing underwater robots to space robots to surgical robots to self-driving cars (also considered to be robots!), Reiley has worked with them all. "I wanted to work in robotics in ways that robots complement humans to make us feel superhuman," she says. "Humans and robots have different strengths and weaknesses, and instead of being scared of robots, we should work together with them to enhance one another."

For example, she helped create the Ion surgical robot, which became available in 2019. The Ion robot gives surgeons "superhuman" abilities. It's a snake-like robot that can enter a person's body through the mouth and then "slither" down the throat and around the lungs. It collects tissue samples from the lungs that doctors can later examine to see if anything is wrong. The special thing about this robot is that it is super-flexible, so it can reach hard-to-get-to places inside the human body (with a surgeon controlling it from a computer console, kind of like a video game). It also "sees" really well—and everything it sees is displayed on a screen that surgeons can look at. Since the bot doesn't make any incisions, Reiley says, "You can walk out a few hours later and feel pretty good."

After working in the medical field for a number of years, Reiley switched gears. She had heard that car crashes are one of the leading causes of accidental death in the United States. The crashes are mostly caused by human error. Many studies show that self-driving cars, on the other hand, are much safer and have a lower rate of accidents. Reiley reasoned that self-driving cars were like preventive medicine—they can help save lives. So she helped start an autonomous car company called Drive.ai.

She was so excited about her new venture that, even though she was getting married that same year, she spent all of her wedding savings to fund the new company. (Don't worry, she still had a beautiful—and small—wedding at a retreat with her family.)

One thing that makes Drive.ai different from other driverless car companies is that she developed ways for the cars to "talk" to humans (like pedestrians and other drivers) and to show emotions. When human drivers are behind the wheel, they can lock eyes with

"DON'T JUST BE A CONSUMER OF TECHNOLOGY— BE A **CREATOR** OF IT."

a bicyclist, signaling that it's safe to cross in front of the car. They can mouth the words "thank you" to another human driver who lets them in their lane. But how does a self-driving car communicate with people? "These are the first robots in the wild," Reiley says about the cars, which use "deep learning" artificial intelligence, meaning they can actually learn stuff and keep improving on their own. "And what's critically missing in the conversation around autonomous vehicles is how do we communicate with them?" Reiley came up with two fun—yet very useful—ways: different beeps to convey different emotions, and LED signs that use emojis. For instance, a car might have a cute "whoop!" sound that means it's safe to cross, while a deeper "whaaa!" might mean you're driving too close behind another car. An LED sign could flash an angry emoji if someone cuts off the car or wave a hand to say "Thanks!"

Once Drive.ai was able to get its cars on the road in a few cities, with plans to keep expanding, Reiley felt it was time to move on. She is currently part of a new health-care company that is inventing something specifically for women. She says for now it's top secret, but "it's a really big idea."

And that's what all of Reiley's projects seem to be: big ideas mixed with futuristic robots that work with humans to help save lives. What better job could a roboticist ask for?

Katherine Johnson

FIGURE OUT WHAT YOU LIKE DOING AND **KEEP DOING IT**

As a girl, Katherine Johnson was fascinated by numbers. "I counted everything," she once said. "I counted the steps to the road, the steps up to church, the number of dishes and silverware I washed . . . anything that could be counted, I did." Not surprisingly, she also loved math. In fact, she liked it so much she became a "human computer" for NASA and helped put the first astronauts up into space—and onto the moon.

Although Johnson was a math major in college—graduating when she was only 18!—she had never imagined that she would be calculating *trajectories*, or flight paths, for space travel. After all, she was born in 1918, and women and African Americans in her generation weren't usually given the chance for such careers. But Johnson's enthusiasm and genius for math made people notice her.

After getting married and having children, a relative told her about a group of black women with math degrees who were working as human computers. (Before electronic computers were widely used, the people who were hired to make mathematical calculations were called *computers*.) They were employed at NACA (National Advisory Committee for Aeronautics), which became NASA in 1958. Johnson applied for a job at NACA in 1952 and was hired a year later.

Known as the West Computers, Johnson and the other women in her group were "working on airplanes," she once said. Why airplanes? "Because when I went there, that's what it was." NACA focused on planes, while it successor, NASA, would focus on rockets. Unfortunately, NACA was segregated, and Johnson's team was treated differently from the white people who worked at the company. The black employees had to use a separate bathroom, which was much farther away from their office than the "white" bathroom, and they were not allowed to eat their lunch in the regular dining room. But even with racism all around her, Johnson says she still enjoyed her job, because she was doing what she loved—working with numbers.

One day, Johnson heard that some of the men were going to special meetings about a space program that the newly formed agency NASA was starting up. She asked if she could go along. One of the men said, "Well, the girls don't usually go." To which she boldly replied, "Well, is there a law?" Finally, the boss just said, "Let her go."

Johnson began attending all of NASA's meetings, and the engineers noticed she could do geometry problems that they couldn't solve. Soon enough she was making important calculations about space travel for NASA (which ended its segregation policy). Her work had to be precise in order to prevent potential disasters. She had to figure out things like the rotation of Earth, exactly what time a rocket would have to leave Earth, what its flight path would

HARDWORKING AND HUMBLE

Although Johnson helped America with some of its proudest achievements, she never bragged. In fact, her children have said that they never knew how important her work was until they read about her. Later in life she won many awards, including the Presidential Medal of Freedom awarded by President Barack Obama in 2015. Hollywood even released a movie called *Hidden Figures* in 2016 about her and her colleagues Dorothy Vaughan and Mary Jackson. She was honored but said the most meaningful awards she ever got were letters from schoolchildren she'd inspired.

be, and where the spacecraft would land. "It was intricate, but it was possible," she later said. Johnson became so important and trusted at NASA that, in 1961, she was the person in charge of computing the trajectory for Alan Shepard, the first American to travel into space.

Around this time, electronic computers became available, so NASA used them to plan astronaut John Glenn's spaceflight. In 1962, he was about to be the first American to orbit Earth. But before the rocket was ready for the launch, Glenn suddenly said he wasn't going—not unless Katherine Johnson first verified that the electronic computers were correct. "If she says they're good," he said, "then I'm ready to go." He trusted her more than a machine! She carefully reviewed the computer's calculations and assured him that he was good to go.

Johnson kept up with the times, learning to use computers, and in 1969, she was the person responsible for mapping the flight path for Apollo 11—the first rocket to take astronauts to the moon!

"MATH HAD ALWAYS COME EASILY TO ME. I LOVED NUMBERS, AND NUMBERS LOVED ME. THEY FOLLOWED ME EVERYWHERE."

Part of Johnson's success, besides the fact that she was incredibly talented with math, could be credited to her curiosity. "I found myself very inquisitive—I wanted to know what was going on—and why," she said in an interview in 2011. But perhaps even more important than curiosity, she always pursued her interest. "The main thing is I liked what I was doing," she has said.

Allie Weber

START WITH THE SMALL PROBLEMS

When Allie Weber was five years old, she wanted to build a robot, but her parents said she was too young. So at age six, she went down to her basement and built one anyway. She recycled a kitty litter box, a cake pan, some pipes, and other household stuff and ended up with a bright red "Robie the Robot" that moved when you pulled a string. It was a fun surprise when it won the science fair! But what came next was completely unexpected.

After Allie's mother proudly posted photos of the winning robot on her blog, a European doll company called Lottie contacted her. They had seen the blog post, were completely impressed, and asked if they could make a doll called Robot Girl based on Allie! Lottie was creating a series of STEM dolls (like Fossil Hunter, Stargazer, and Wildlife Photographer), and Robot Girl would be their first one. Launched in 2013, the doll (which is no longer available) looked like Allie and had a robot companion (based on Robie, of course) called Busy Lizzie.

Winning the fair and then working with a doll company charged Allie, from South Dakota, with inspiration. Suddenly she began to invent things nonstop, all while she was in elementary and middle school. She built a solar-powered dollhouse with a real wind turbine and a gorilla-shaped "goal-rilla soccer trainer" that hangs from the top bar of the goal and substitutes as a goalie during soccer practice. She also created a dart game for children who need their lungs tested. The patients blow into a tube that shoots darts, making the procedure fun instead of scary. These are just a few of her clever inventions.

And by age 10, she'd invented something that would earn her her first patent! (A *patent* is a special document from the government that says your invention is original, and nobody else can make and sell it without your permission.) It was for the Frost Stopper—a glove that warns you when your hands are in danger of *frostbite* (damage to the skin caused by exposure to freezing cold temperatures). Allie got the idea one snowy winter after she had been sledding with her cousins. "I noticed at first that my fingers stung a little bit, which was probably a bad sign," she says, but she was having too much fun to go inside. Her fingers then went numb. By the time she got home, she had frostbite on her pinkie, which inspired her to invent something to prevent this from happening again.

First Allie attached a temperature sensor to a glove. The sensor is powered by an *Arduino* (a small electronic device that allows you to add sound, motion, light, and other interactive things to your projects). Then she connected the Arduino, which she programmed to beep, to a winter hat with built-in headphones. If the glove got too cold for too long, the wearer would hear beeping through the headphones. "It will keep on beeping until you warm up. It annoys you into being safe," she says.

Making the gloves definitely had its challenges. "One time I mixed up whether my sensor was digital or analog when I put it together, so when I put the glove on to try it out, the sensor got really hot and burned my finger!" she says. "It was kind of the opposite of the frostbite problem. But after learning from my mistakes many times, I was finally able to create a working prototype that I was proud of." The Frost Stopper won the 2016 Spark!Lab Global Invent It Challenge.

At age 14, Allie already has more experience as an inventor than many adult scientists do. She says one thing that has made her successful is staying realistic. "When people think of problems, they often think of huge things like world hunger or cancer . . . and they are often too much for a beginner." Allie says it's better to "start with the little things in your own life. Even if you have a problem that no one else has, if you create an invention

> **"YOU DON'T ALWAYS NEED TO START BY SOLVING THE BIG PROBLEMS— A COMBINATION OF LITTLE PROBLEMS BEING SOLVED MIGHT LEAD UP TO THE BIG SOLUTION."**

for it, you are immediately making your life a whole lot easier." When asked what she wants to do in the future, Allie's answer is always the same: "Kids are not 'the future,' we are here now. We are not going to change the world 'someday,' we are already doing it."

Adriana Ocampo

LOOK FOR **EVIDENCE** TO SUPPORT NEW THEORIES

Although Adriana Ocampo was born in Colombia, she grew up in Argentina, where she loved to sit on the roof of her house at night with her dog, Tauro (named after the constellation Taurus). "The stars were fascinating," she says. "I wondered about those lights—what were they? How far away? Were there people like us there?"

In 1969, Ocampo's friends gathered around the only black-and-white television in the neighborhood to watch the moon landing. "I wanted to be part of NASA, because it was an example that dreams can really come true," she says. So at age 14, when her family moved to the United States, the first thing she did when she landed at the airport was ask a customs agent, "Where is NASA?" Two and a half years later, she began volunteering at NASA during the summer. She was later hired as a technical aide, and she continued to work there through college. After she graduated, she got a permanent job as a planetary geologist at NASA (where she still works today).

During Ocampo's early years at NASA, scientists debated about how dinosaurs became extinct. The common theory was that around 66 million years ago, a series of massive volcanoes erupted, which sent enough gas, ash, and particles into the atmosphere to block out the sun, killing off the prehistoric creatures. But, in 1980, some scientists discovered that the ocean floor was covered in *iridium*—

a silvery metal that is rare on Earth's surface but commonly found in asteroids. This led some scientists—including Ocampo—to believe that a catastrophic asteroid was actually to blame for the extinction.

But the asteroid theory needed more proof. If such a destructive asteroid did indeed strike Earth, where was the *impact crater* (the hole or dent left in Earth from being hit by the gargantuan asteroid)? Nobody knew.

One day, Ocampo attended a science convention and saw a slideshow by an archaeologist who was looking for evidence of Mayan canals near Chicxulub (pronounced CHEEK-shoe-loob), Mexico. While looking at the slides, she noticed something in the background of some of the images: mysterious sinkholes that formed a perfect semicircle on the Yucatán Peninsula. She perked up. Her first thought was that the arc of sinkholes looked like the partial outline of an impact crater—and the other half would be buried under the ocean. After the talk, she excitedly asked the presenter, "Do you know what makes up this ring?" He shook his head. "No, I have no idea." Then she asked, "Have you thought of the possibility of an impact crater?" And he said, "No, what's that?"

Ocampo knew she was onto something, but stayed calm. "As soon as I saw the slides, that was my 'aha! moment,'" she later told the BBC. "I was really excited inside, but I kept cool because obviously you don't know until you have more evidence." Ocampo spoke with other scientists, who had also suspected this was an impact crater.

"ANYBODY WHO IS A GOOD OBSERVER AND USES HER OR HIS IMAGINATION IS A SCIENTIST."

As a team, they collected more evidence. From satellite images, they learned that the ring of sinkholes indeed made a complete circle that measured more than 100 miles across. They also found small pieces of *tektites*—black glass made from molten rock created by meteors—spread around the planet. These rocks dated back to the same time that the dinosaurs became extinct.

Like connecting a jigsaw puzzle, the scientists all brought their own pieces of evidence to the table, until Ocampo put them all together and had enough proof to back up the theory: the asteroid that caused the Chicxulub crater—nicknamed the Crater of Doom—had caused the extinction of dinosaurs. As with most major discoveries, it took a while to convince the science world, but after two years, she was able to get her findings published in the science journal *Nature*. Today, many scientists agree that both theories might be right—dinosaurs were likely wiped out by a one-two punch from volcanoes *and* the asteroid that created the Chicxulub crater.

Ocampo, who won the National Hispanic Scientist of the Year award in 2016, is now in charge of NASA's mission to Jupiter *and* its mission to Pluto. She is also keeping an eye on an asteroid called Bennu, which could possibly collide with Earth in about 200 years. She and her team are researching ways to push Bennu out of orbit.

Ocampo, who has always dreamed big, looks forward to "the first interplanetary footprint on Mars being from a woman." And she offers this challenge to girls interested in space exploration: "Be bold, think big, and be part of the crew to Mars." And whether it's traveling to Mars or achieving any kind of goal, "the key is to work hard—and never, *never* give up on your dreams."

Simone Giertz

EMBRACE FAILURE AND BOREDOM AS INGREDIENTS FOR SUCCESS

When Simone Giertz first launched her YouTube channel, she was doing comedy skits. She's really funny, but she didn't have many viewers. So, in 2015, after two and a half years, she tried something different. She showed off a silly robot she built—a helmet with a toothbrush attached to it that flips down and frantically brushes your teeth (and, accidentally, your cheeks!). The video went viral, her subscriber count shot up, and Giertz's life completely changed.

Giertz (pronounced Yetch), who grew up in Sweden, always wanted to be an inventor or a scientist. But as a perfectionist who cried in high school over getting a B on a math test, she was also terribly afraid of failure. In fact, failing "was my biggest fear at the time," she later said in a TED Talk. At first, her fear of failure paralyzed her. She couldn't invent anything, because "building things . . . especially if you're teaching yourself . . . has a high likelihood of failure," she explained. But one day, she had a brilliant idea: she decided to flip failure on its head and fail *on purpose* by building useless inventions. "Instead of trying to succeed, I was going to try to build things that would fail," she said at TED 2018. "For the first time in my life, I did not have to deal with my performance anxiety."

Instead, "that pressure quickly got replaced by enthusiasm, and it allowed me to just play."

After her successful toothbrush helmet video in 2015, Giertz became famous on YouTube as an "inventor of useless things," as she has called herself. Without an engineering degree, Giertz learned how to build her robots by watching YouTube videos. "I never sat down with a book, being like, 'okay, now I'm going to learn about transistors,'" she has said. Instead, she googled the tutorials she needed to learn as she built things.

Every month or two, she posted a new wacky contraption she had invented. For example, there was the "breakfast machine," a robotic arm that pours cereal and milk into a bowl—and (oops!) everywhere else—and then attempts to spoon-feed you. There was also the "wake-up machine," a rubber hand that hangs over your bed and slaps you in the face to wake you up, and the "chopping machine," a pair of medieval-looking knives that chop vegetables—or your fingers if you're not careful! These quirky inventions got her noticed, and soon she was invited to speak at a TED event, be a guest on *The Late Show with Stephen Colbert*, and even cohost with *MythBusters*'s Adam Savage on his video channel *Tested*. Giertz's success was like a dream come true for any budding inventor. And then she got some terrible news.

In April 2018, at age 27, she announced on her channel that she had a brain tumor "the size of a golf ball." Although she was terrified,

TED: IDEAS WORTH SPREADING

TED is an exciting series of short, smart, thought-provoking talks. Although TED used to stand for Technology, Entertainment, and Design, it's opened up to include nature, offbeat science, fashion, medicine, gaming, and more. Many women in this book have given a TED Talk (Sarah Parcak, Temple Grandin, Martine Rothblatt, and others). TED Talks, like Giertz's 2018 presentation, "Why You Should Make Useless Things," take place in Vancouver, Canada, where TED is based. TEDx events happen all over the world. Although most TED and TEDx speakers are adults, plenty are teenagers too (like Keiana Cavé and Gitanjali Rao, who are also featured in this book!), which goes to show you that you're never too young for great ideas. For more information, go to ted.com.

she joked, "I don't even like golf." She said she was getting "extensive brain surgery" and later tweeted that she'd given the tumor a name—Brian the Brain Tumor. Nearly three months later, Giertz let her fans know that she had made it through surgery and was feeling good—then the following January, she announced that the tumor had come back. But, as she deals with it, she says she doesn't want people to pity her. "I don't want to be brain tumor girl," she says on her channel. She wants to be the "builder girl who can build whatever she wants."

And that's exactly who she is as she continues to invent awesome things. In fact, by summer 2019, she and her team built something way beyond useless and into the realm of amazing. She converted a red Tesla Model 3 (a planet-friendly, ultramodern, all-electric car) into a pickup truck, which she named Truckla—"my ultimate dream car." She posted the process on her channel, and the video got nearly 10 million views in five months. "It's definitely the biggest project that we've ever taken on."

So how does she come up with all of her ideas? According to Giertz, it's important to get bored. "Being bored is one of my best creative processes," she has said. It "makes me really want to create things and entertain myself." Another strategy is to get off the Internet. "I just get off all screens and try to remember what I used to do before I had those things." It's when she's not overwhelmed with a million things to do that her best ideas come.

Budding inventors and robot fans can enjoy her kid-friendly videos on GoldieBlox's YouTube channel.

"BUILDING STUPID THINGS WAS ACTUALLY QUITE SMART."

MASSACHVSETTS INSTITVTE OF TECHNOLOGY

Shirley Ann Jackson

PAVE THE WAY FOR
FUTURE SCIENTISTS

Shirley Ann Jackson, born in Washington, DC, has made scientific discoveries that are helping to change computers in unimaginable ways. The first African American woman to receive the National Medal of Science, she has worked in scientific development and in government, and she is now president of a technology college in New York. Although her career has been a tech-girl's dream, it didn't come easy: she had to battle sexist and racist attitudes along the way.

As a child, Jackson would catch bumblebees to study their behavior. She was always fascinated with how things worked. So when she was accepted to MIT in 1964, she was thrilled! But her excitement soon turned to loneliness. Making friends was hard. It was bad enough that there were only 24 other women in her class, as opposed to 874 men. Even worse, she was the *only* African American in the physics department. In the dining hall, the other women wouldn't sit with her. When she tried to join a group of women studying in her dorm, they were cruel and told her to leave. Jackson ran to her room and cried. But with a lot of homework to do, she soon dried her eyes and got back to her studies.

Rather than give up and go home, she was determined to make MIT a more diverse place. In 1968, after Martin Luther King Jr. was assassinated, she co-founded the Black Student Union, which gave

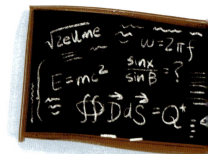

African Americans a place to unite at school. She also began helping people of color apply to MIT. In one year, MIT's enrollment of African American freshman went from 5 to 57, and the numbers continued to climb.

In 1973, Jackson graduated with a PhD in physics, becoming the first black woman to earn a doctorate at MIT. She then worked at AT&T Bell Laboratories from 1976 to 1991 as a *theoretical physicist*—someone who uses math instead of tools like telescopes to figure out how nature works. At Bell, she researched the way light and electricity behave inside layers of crystals and on the surface of liquid helium. Her discoveries helped pave the way for breakthroughs in cutting-edge technologies like *quantum computers*—futuristic supercomputers that will run so fast and be so powerful that they'll be able to do things barely imaginable today. IBM and Microsoft are currently working on ways to build them. Jackson also worked in the White House—twice! President Bill Clinton hired her as the first woman and the first African American to chair the US Nuclear Regulatory Commission (which ensures the safe use of nuclear energy). And President Barack Obama hired her as one of his advisors on science and technology issues.

In 1999, Jackson became the first woman and the first African American president of Rensselaer Polytechnic Institute (RPI), a leading university of technology. She has improved classes, campus life, and diversity at the university. Last year, when speaking to RPI's graduating class, she gave advice that perfectly sums up how she has led her own life: "Never allow anyone, or anything, to undermine your confidence. You all have the potential to build unique careers and to uplift lives."

"I HAD MANY DAYS OF MY OWN SELF-DOUBT, BUT I'VE ALWAYS BEEN WILLING TO TRY."

Sumita Mitra

BE **CURIOUS** AND ASK A LOT OF QUESTIONS

In ancient times, if someone was missing a tooth, they might replace it with a seashell, a bit of metal, or even a piece of animal bone. Of course, dentistry greatly improved over the centuries, but until the 1990s, cavities were still filled with silver metal, and fake teeth often looked fake. Then chemist Sumita Mitra invented a substance that transformed dentistry—and people's smiles.

When Mitra first took a job in the dental materials division at 3M (a huge manufacturing company famous for making Scotch tape and Post-it Notes), she had no experience with dentistry. But she was a chemist with a lot of ideas, and 3M wanted inquisitive researchers like her to create new technologies and products for them. While exploring what kinds of products dentists needed, Mitra became interested in *nanoparticles*, bits of matter so small they are invisible to the human eye (because they are smaller than the wavelength of visible light). She knew that nanoparticles are extremely strong and wondered if nanoparticles were made into tooth fillings, would their special optical properties keep them looking smooth even after wear and tear in the mouth? Could the combination of nanoparticles' appearance and strength make them a perfect material for teeth?

This was in the 1990s, when nanotechnology was just emerging as a field and hadn't really been applied to dentistry yet. In fact, it

was so new that nanoparticles were scarce. So if Mitra was actually going to pursue her idea, she would first have to convince 3M to build equipment that could make enough nanoparticles to experiment with. "There was really no methodology available to do this in large scale because it hadn't been done before," she says. "We had to manufacture very large amounts, which was very challenging."

Because this was such a futuristic—and costly—idea, "not everyone was convinced," she says. But a few people at 3M were excited enough to give it a shot, including some scientists on her team. So, with great teamwork, they experimented over and over again, combining *nanoclusters* (groups of nanoparticles that look like bunches of grapes) with particles of *nanomeric silica* (a hard, colorless chemical compound) in every way possible. They also designed the equipment to manufacture the material.

Finally, after three and a half years, Mitra and her team had reason to celebrate. They were the first to invent and commercialize a dental filling material with nanoparticles. Up until then, materials to restore teeth were either attractive but weak (meaning they chipped easily) or they were strong but didn't look as good. Mitra's invention was a tooth-colored substance that was both extremely durable and looked like natural teeth. They called it Filtek Supreme Universal Restorative. Now it is in most dentist offices and has fixed more than 600 million smiles worldwide!

"IF THERE ARE ROADBLOCKS, TAKE A DETOUR."

Mitra is retired now but keeps busy mentoring kids in science. She says curiosity is the first step in becoming an inventor. "Ask questions and don't take anything for granted," she advises. Questions like *How does it work?* and *How can we make it better?* are a great place to start. "Just get active," she says. "Get your fingers wet, and go for it."

Michelle Oblak

EXPERIMENT WITH 3-D PRINTING— AND SAVE ANIMALS' LIVES

Patches is a lovable pooch, a dachshund that looks like a happy hot dog. Her life was great until a bump appeared on the top of her head. At first, the veterinarian who saw her wasn't too concerned. But then the bump started to grow and grow until it was the size of an orange! The vet told her worried family that nothing could be done for Patches. Fortunately, her family kept searching. They eventually found Dr. Michelle Oblak, who—with the help of a 3-D printer—saved Patches's life.

Oblak is a cat and dog surgeon who specializes in helping pets with cancer. She lives in Canada. After she got the call from a vet in the United States, describing how enormous Patches's tumor was, she was optimistic that she could help. She flew to New York to meet "Little Unicorn," which was what Patches's family was now affectionately calling her. "Patches was a really sweet, happy-go-lucky little dachshund. She was just loving life," Oblak says. "And her family was absolutely amazing. They loved her to bits and wanted to do anything they could to improve her life."

As luck would have it, Oblak had been preparing for a case like this. "I'm always trying to figure out how we can do something better. I look at the different aspects of procedures we do and try to see how I can improve them," she says. "And one area I thought we were not doing as well as we could was with skull surgery." The problem with removing a large tumor from a pet's head is that it leaves a hole where part of the skull has been removed. This means the brain is left unprotected. Sometimes the skull is fixed (which takes a second surgery) with a one-size-fits-all *imitation plate*, or skull cap, but because dogs' heads vary so much in size and shape (think of the difference between a Chihuahua and a German shepherd!), it rarely fits right. The new plate can change the appearance of the dog's face and head.

But Oblak was prepared for the challenge. "The great thing was, I was in the middle of doing a research project, looking at ways to use 3-D printing to repair skulls. Because even though we would hopefully remove the tumor, it was going to leave a really big hole behind," she says. "I thought 3-D printing would be the *perfect* way to repair the hole created from removing the tumor." Perfect because, with 3-D printing, you can tell a computer precisely what size and shape you want something to be, and it will build it right in front of you.

"3-D PRINTING HAS OPENED UP SO MANY DOORS—AND WE DON'T EVEN KNOW YET HOW FAR IT CAN GO. IT'S ONLY LIMITED TO OUR IMAGINATIONS."

But it's not like Oblak could just grab a tape measure to figure out the exact dimensions of the dog's skull. Instead, Patches had to get a *CT scan*—a process that takes a bunch of X-rays at once to give detailed pictures of what's inside a body without having to cut it open. Oblak then put the CT scan into a special computer program that showed every angle and dimension inside the dog's head. She fed these measurements into a 3-D printer, which created a skull plate using a super-strong, super-light metal material called titanium. In fact, she says the titanium skull was "as light as a cracker."

All this technology allowed Oblak and her colleague, Dr. Galina Hayes, to "plan how we were going to perform surgery" beforehand, from removing the tumor to replacing the skull. "We actually practiced the surgery virtually, ahead of time," Oblak says. And the practice paid off. The surgery for Patches took only four hours—much less time than it would normally take for an animal doctor to remove the tumor and then repair the skull without a 3-D printer. And "the day after surgery, she was already going out for a walk and wagging her tail and sniffing the grass and all that kind of stuff," Oblak says.

Ever since she was a young child, Oblak wanted to be a vet. "I always felt a deep connection to working with animals," she says. For young people who have the same dream, she says to always explore, ask questions, and look for ways to improve things around you. "I'm always looking at how to do something faster, more efficiently, less painfully," she says. And it looks like that is exactly what she did for "Titanium Top," which is Patches's *new* nickname.

Star Simpson

IF IT DOESN'T EXIST, **INVENT IT**

One of the great things about being an engineer is that if you want something that doesn't exist, you can just make it. And that's exactly what Star Simpson is good at doing.

Born in Hawaii, Simpson says one of her first—and favorite—inventions came to her when she was around 10 years old because she hated sweeping the driveway. It was a Saturday chore that she dreaded, because her driveway was long and steep, and it took her about an hour to sweep it clean. She wondered how she could do it more quickly, and then an idea hit her. She gathered all of the extension cords in her house, connected them to a small electric fan, and hopped on her skateboard. She then blew the leaves off her driveway as she slowly rolled down the hill. And voilà! She finished her chore in no time—and had fun as well.

It was with this same clever thinking that she came up with one of her more popular inventions. She was 18 and a new electrical engineering student at MIT when she saw students playing with drones. While watching them, a few things popped into her head at once. She wondered what kind of positive thing she could do with drones. She also remembered how slow mail was in Hawaii and thought delivery drones sounded like a pretty nice idea. And speaking of delivery . . . she thought, "If I could have a taco right now, how great would that be?"

Then came her "aha! moment": drones + tacos = TacoCopter! By combining *quadcopters* (helicopter-like drones with four propellers), a smartphone with GPS, and, of course, delicious tacos with a newly made TacoCopter website, she figured out how to create a service that could actually land tacos on your doorstep. Although her TacoCopter website got picked up by the news and was liked on Facebook more than 14,000 times, Simpson says it was never a serious business— a bunch of delivery drones flying all over the place would be too dangerous. She just wanted to explore the possibility of future delivery drones.

Simpson is an engineer who teaches herself by inventing things. "The main reason I've built most things," she said, "is because I wanted to learn. I wanted to understand something better." And she's constantly making new things. Besides her quirky inventions (like the leaf blower and the TacoCopter), Simpson has created dozens of other things that she thought the world could use, such as Circuit Classics (a cool electronics kit for beginners), Tether-tenna (a helicopter drone made for Facebook that brings Internet access to underserved areas), and a tactile 3-D puzzle (like a Rubik's Cube) that blind or visually impaired people can play with.

> "WHEN YOU'RE JUST GETTING STARTED, YOU MIGHT END UP JUST PUTTING PARTS TOGETHER AND SEEING WHAT THEY DO. IT WON'T ALWAYS WORK. **THAT'S GOOD!**"

One of her most popular creations is both quirky *and* meaningful. When she was working at a lab in San Francisco, DARPA (part of the US Department of Defense) announced that it was looking for proposals from people who could make something that could fly into remote villages, drop off small needed supplies, and then, like magic, disappear into thin air. Yes, they were serious! "The idea was to help people who are in a part of the world that is hard to ship things to by sending them bandages or batteries or other things they might need that are hard to get," says Simpson. So she applied. And she and her team met the challenge! They designed a small glider called APSARA (Aerial Platform Supporting Autonomous Resupply Actions) that can be dropped out of planes above villages in need. (The name refers to a female cloud spirit in Buddhist and Hindu mythology.)

The gliders will be made out of a cardboard-like material called *lignin* (a cross between paper and fabric), which has been soaked with mushroom spores. Before being dropped from a plane, the gliders will be spritzed with liquid, which activates the spores. The spores slowly begin to eat the gliders and, a week after they've landed and dropped off supplies, the gliders will be completely gobbled up, with only a few traces left behind (and DARPA is working on eliminating those traces too).

Simpson, who mentors teenage girls interested in going to MIT, says she feels lucky that she grew up in a rural area of Hawaii, because it allowed her to follow her interests without a lot of people telling her that technology was for boys. Her message to young girls is, "You can be as technical as you want to be. Nobody else can decide what technical skills you're allowed to have." And it's your technical skills, along with your imagination, that will allow you to invent any idea you dream up.

LEARNING TO FLY

From the TacoCopter to Tether-tenna to APSARA, Simpson works with a lot of things that fly. In fact, she's also a pilot who flies real gliders! "I wanted to build flying things, so I purposely got my pilot's license as a way of educating myself," she explains. She says getting her license was the best way to really learn about *aerodynamics* (how moving objects are affected by the air around them). And now she loves flying in her spare time. "You're in charge of wherever you want to go," she says. "It's an incredible experience."

Pauline van Dongen

MIX ART AND SCIENCE

Pauline van Dongen is a Dutch fashion designer with a unique workspace, or "playground," as she calls it. Yes, it has a sewing machine, a cutting table, fabric, and an ironing board. But it also has a lab that is decked out with soldering tools, a laser cutter, a 3-D printer, a heat press, LED lights, wires, and other electronics. That's because the clothes she designs not only look great, they also *do* things, like charge phones, light up in the dark, and catch you if you fall.

Van Dongen began experimenting with clothing as a student. While studying fashion, she says she created "the first fully 3-D printed shoe design in the world." And she says she knew soon after becoming a fashion designer that she wanted to create eco-friendly fabrics and explore new materials. She was interested in "looking into what we could do with technology and how technology can change how we relate to the world through our clothes."

Around the same time, her father gave her a light-up running bracelet to wear at night, but she didn't like it. She said it felt scratchy, had weak batteries, and looked "geeky." She tweaked it with fabric and LEDs until it looked good, felt good, and functioned beautifully. This was a turning point for van Dongen. In 2010, she opened a studio to specialize in *wearable technology*, or fashion that merges technology with design. Since she hadn't studied engineering in school, she had to learn about electronics by collaborating with engineers, including someone she described as a "robot hacker," who taught her about circuit boards and software.

One of her first garments was a short black dress that had 72 small solar panels on the front and back, arranged in two columns that resembled shiny suspenders. If worn in the sun for at least an hour, the dress, which had a built-in charger, could power up a phone to 50 percent. A big challenge when creating this solar-powered dress, which was just a prototype, was figuring out how people could wash it without hurting all the wiring hidden inside. "It wasn't as practical in the beginning," van Dongen says. "You could wear it, but it couldn't be washed."

She began to explore other ways to design with solar technology. She experimented with what she later called the Solar Shirt—a dark blue T-shirt that displayed a geometric design made with 120 super-thin *solar cells* (small solar panels) ironed on. Combining the solar cells with *printed electronics* (materials made by printing electrical circuits instead of ink) turned the electronic circuit into something "very flexible and stretchable, and it created a graphic texture," she says. In other words, the technology also became the design!

The T-shirt looked awesome and could charge all kinds of devices, from phones to MP3 players to cameras. But it still wasn't easy to wash. The T-shirt did, however, get her noticed in the new wearable tech market. Big companies started asking her to design high-tech clothing or invent high-tech materials for them.

The last few years have been busy for van Dongen, whose astonishing projects include solar-powered windbreakers for nature guides in the northern islands of the Netherlands, light-up running shirts, a denim jacket that reminds you to be present by gently stroking your back, a sensor-embedded undershirt that softly vibrates when you're slouching, and a headband studded with infrared LEDs to reduce anxiety and stress.

Along with smart wearables, she's also developing smart materials by weaving tiny solar beads right into the threads that make fabric. "I'm really fascinated with the idea that, not just clothing, but textiles in general can generate energy," she says. She's already worked with a company to make a backpack with a strap made from solar material. Hikers can plug their devices into the strap for a charge, even if they're in the middle of nowhere (as long as there's a bit of sun!).

For artists and designers who are also interested in STEM, van Dongen says it's important to keep an open mind—and stay curious. Mixing up science and art can spur new and unexpected innovations. If she'd had a closed mind about her future, she would not be revolutionizing the world of fashion with technology. "Discover your path without already mapping out where exactly you're heading," she says. "You have to have *some* strategy, but you shouldn't overthink too much, because in the end, your path will change along the way."

TURN YOUR LAB INTO A PLAYGROUND

Wearable technology is so new that oftentimes a client comes up with a brand-new idea, "and I don't even know exactly how I'm going to make it," van Dongen says. For instance, a company recently asked her to design (and engineer!) a balance-tracking belt geared for older people that will inflate into an airbag and act as a cushion if the person falls. The challenge of figuring out how to make these projects work—while still looking stylish—is what makes her job so rewarding. "My studio is really a playground," she says. "There's a lot of things I have never done before, because it's something so new, so I give myself the time and space to explore. It's *fun*."

Maria Andrade

USE FOOD SCIENCE TO
SAVE LIVES

As a young girl in Cape Verde, a small island country off the coast of mainland Africa, Maria Andrade imagined her future. "I had a dream," she says. "I told my mother when I was five years old, 'I don't want to be baking in the house. I want to do something bigger.'" She wanted to help grow coffee—until she learned about a more powerful crop: a special potato that could save millions of children from blindness and even death.

After studying plant genetics at the University of Arizona in the 1980s, Andrade landed a job in Cape Verde, where she was asked to work with *maize*, or corn. But growing lots of maize didn't make sense to her. Her country was very hot and dry, and it often suffered through droughts, which killed many of the corn crops. Farmers in Cape Verde needed to grow a food that was *drought-tolerant*, which means it doesn't need much water or rain. She worried about all the children in Africa who were suffering from *malnutrition* (a severe condition caused by a lack of healthy food). In the country of Mozambique, for instance, nearly 70 percent of young children weren't getting enough vitamin A, causing many of them to be sick, go blind, and even die. It was obvious to Andrade that the country needed to grow a crop packed with vitamin A and other nutrients.

Then she learned about orange flesh sweet potatoes. If the center of a potato is orange, it's a "powerful tool," says Andrade, because not only is it packed with vitamin A, but it's also a sturdy plant that grows in extremely dry weather. And it grows fast.

Andrade got her PhD in plant breeding from North Carolina State University in 1994 and then moved to Mozambique. "When I moved to Mozambique 23 years ago, there was no orange flesh sweet potato," she says. "I had to introduce them and start breeding them." She set up a farm, a lab, and a kitchen. Out in the field, she breeds her sweet potatoes to make them richer in vitamin A, more drought-tolerant, and tastier. In the lab, she examines her potatoes to see "how much iron, zinc, and beta-carotene" they contain. (*Beta-carotene* is a substance that human bodies convert into vitamin A.) She also tests their dryness, "because a sweet potato that's watery is not the taste of Africa. Nobody will like it."

In the kitchen, Andrade invites people to test the different types of sweet potatoes she's grown. "We boil the sweet potatoes and let people come and do what we call the 'palatability test' to assess if they like it or not," she says. "They look at how nice the color is, the consistency, how sweet it is, and how dry it is." This helps Andrade know which potatoes will have the best chance at success at the market or in a grocery store.

It took Andrade about five years to grow, breed, and finally present her sweet potatoes to the world. Her delicious, vitamin-rich, drought-tolerant potatoes were nearly perfect (although she is constantly improving her potatoes). But this is when she found out

"IF YOU HAVE TO STEP THOUSANDS OF TIMES GOING AFTER WHAT YOU WANT, TAKE THOSE STEPS."

her biggest challenge was not the science. It was people's perception! "It was very, very hard to convince people to eat sweet potatoes," she says. Nobody wanted them at first. Most Africans liked only white potatoes, which don't have the vitamin A they desperately needed. In fact, they were embarrassed to eat sweet potatoes in public, "because it wasn't a priority crop," so people would think "you had to be very poor to be eating sweet potatoes in Mozambique."

But instead of giving up, Andrade got really creative: she turned the country orange. She made orange skirts that had sweet potato messages on them for people living in villages. She also replaced her own wardrobe with orange clothes. "I don't have any other color of clothes," she says. She promoted sweet potatoes on the radio, through street performances, and by passing out interesting recipes for dishes like ice cream, bread, fries, and even birthday cakes made

with orange sweet potatoes. She even painted sweet potatoes on cars! Every driver on her farm had a car makeover. "I immediately painted them orange— our work cars, our pickups, our trucks, our normal cars."

Suddenly, her potatoes took off. Interest in them spread not only throughout Mozambique but also across Africa. "Now, deep in the villages, I see children eating sweet potatoes," she says. And the children "look better, because they are getting vitamins." In fact, Andrade's sweet potatoes have made such a huge impact on fighting malnutrition that she won the prestigious 2016 World Food Prize.

She reminds anyone who wants to improve the world to take it one step at a time. "Success is a combination of so many small successes. Don't be lazy, don't waste time, and be persistent," she says. "But first, you need a dream."

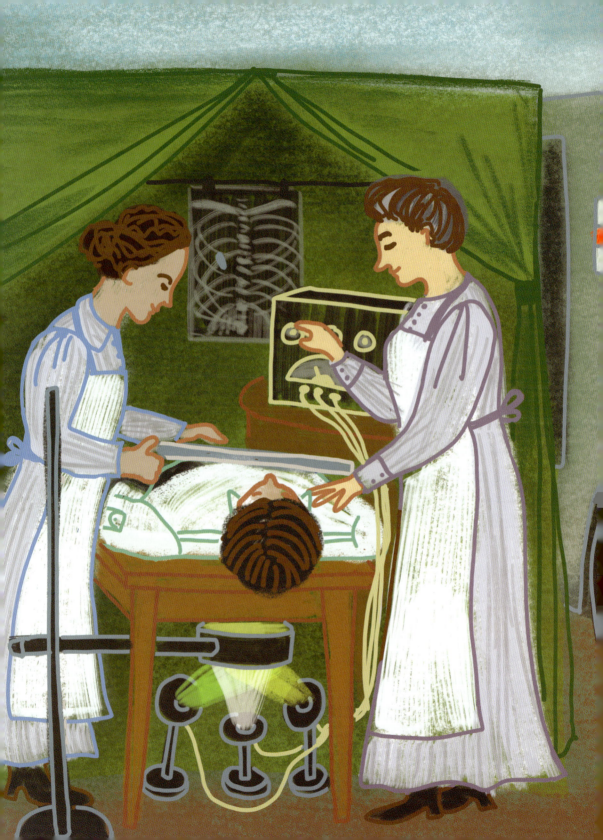

Marie Curie

TAKE YOUR DISCOVERIES OUT OF THE LAB AND **INTO THE FIELD**

Marie Curie, one of the world's most famous scientists, was born in Warsaw, Poland, in 1867. This was a time when most scientists were men, but that didn't stop her from making discoveries that would change the world.

Curie's original name was Maria Sklodowska, and as a child she went by the nickname Manya. The youngest of five children, she often took long walks with her father, a physics and math teacher. They enthusiastically chatted about the nature around them and, by the time she was a teenager, she wanted to be a scientist. She graduated high school at the young age of 15 but couldn't attend the university in Warsaw because they didn't admit women (it was common for universities to be boys-only clubs in those days). So she and her sister Bronia cooked up a plan. She would work to pay for her sister's schooling. And then Bronia would do the same for her. After four long years, Curie traveled to France at age 24 to attend the University of Paris, also known as the Sorbonne. There, she changed her name to Marie to sound more French.

Curie studied so hard she sometimes forgot to eat, but she said she was very happy, because studying chemistry and physics was her passion. And her passion led to some extraordinary accomplishments! In 1898, Curie (who was now married to scientist

Pierre Curie) made two huge breakthroughs while studying uranium ore for her thesis. She discovered elements that actually glowed! First, she found *polonium* (which she named after her home country, Poland). Then, five months later, she identified another glow-in-the-dark element, *radium* (which she and Pierre named after the Latin word *radius*, which means "rays.") These fascinating elements were emitting rays of energy, which inspired her to coin the term "radioactivity."

> **"I AM AMONG THOSE WHO THINK THAT SCIENCE HAS GREAT BEAUTY."**

It took many more years to scientifically prove radium's existence, but her "theory of radioactivity" earned her the 1903 Nobel Prize in Physics. She shared the award with her husband and their colleague Henri Becquerel. Thus, Curie became the first woman to ever win a Nobel Prize.

Marie and Pierre Curie were now wildly famous, with offers of book deals, lectures, and interviews coming at them from all directions. Although this might sound fabulous—and it was!—it was also a little daunting for them, since they truly enjoyed the solitude of spending time by themselves in their lab and studying science together. However, with two daughters and much success, their lives were better than they had ever expected. Until, in 1906, tragedy struck. Pierre was hit by a horse-drawn wagon and died at the age of 46. Curie lost her work partner, her best friend, and her loving husband. Although she was devastated, Curie wasn't about to abandon her love of science.

Curie continued to study radium and polonium, and in 1911, she won her second Nobel Prize, this time in Chemistry, for her discovery of these elements. Curie was the first person (man or woman) to receive two Nobel Prizes! She is still the only woman who has accomplished this. She was also the first person—and only woman—to ever receive a Nobel Prize in two categories (chemistry and physics). The first woman professor at the Sorbonne, Curie taught physics, and scientists and academics from around the world traveled to Paris to listen to her lectures.

Later, Curie used her genius to help more than one million soldiers in World War I. She created a mobile X-ray machine called a "petite Curie," which she and her 17-year-old-daughter, Irène (who later won her own Nobel Prize in Chemistry!), brought to the front line. They made 20 of these units and taught 150 women how to use them to locate bullets and tiny bits of metal embedded in wounded soldiers. This saved countless lives during the war.

Through her work on radioactivity, Curie concluded that radiation could kill healthy—as well as unhealthy—human cells. This led to the development of radiation treatment for cancer, which has saved millions of lives. But ironically, radiation is what killed her. In 1934, at age 66, Curie died of leukemia after many years of radiation exposure.

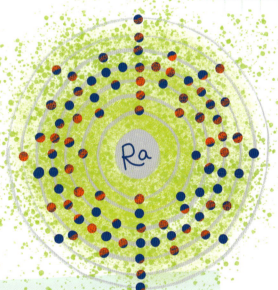

THEORY OF RADIOACTIVITY

Ever since the time of the ancient Greeks, scientists believed that atoms could not be broken or split. (In fact, the Greek word for *atom* means "indivisible.") But certain kinds of atoms produce energy, and Marie Curie realized that when these atoms release that energy, they must change in some way. After doing a lot of research, she came up with the *theory of radioactivity*, which explains that atoms emit particles, and it's these particles that produce the energy, which shows up as glowing rays. She called this energy *radioactivity*.

Jane ní Dhulchaointigh

PLAY, EXPERIMENT, AND LET THE INVENTION **COME TO YOU**

Great inventions sometimes come when you least expect them. And that's how it happened for Jane ní Dhulchaointigh. Little did she know when she was experimenting in art school that she would soon become the inventor of Sugru, a moldable glue, and the founder of a multimillion-dollar company!

Brought up on a farm in rural Ireland, ní Dhulchaointigh (pronounced Nee GUL-queen-tig) had never dreamed of becoming an inventor. She enjoyed art and sculpture and loved to embroider and dye clothes, so she decided to study product design at the Royal College of Art in London. "I really wanted my creativity to make a difference somehow, and product design seemed like a good place to start," she says.

One day at school, ní Dhulchaointigh's professor gave her class an assignment: start experimenting with things to get ideas for a product that you will design. "I thought, 'Okay, I'll start with materials, and maybe that will lead me to some useful ideas,'" she says. She grabbed all kinds of things—sponges, foam, wood, plastics—and broke them all apart. She then smushed them back together in different ways to see what kinds of textures and different looks she could get out of them.

For days she experimented with various materials, until she took some rubbery silicone and mixed it up with sawdust that she found in the wood workshop. Having fun with the putty-like texture, she rolled her concoction up into balls and set them on the side of a workbench before going to lunch. When she returned, she picked up the balls and was surprised to find how much firmer they had become. "Something told me to bang the ball on the ground, and it bounced like a Ping-Pong ball," she says. "And I thought, 'This is so cool! This ball looks like wood, but it bounces like crazy!'"

Ní Dhulchaointigh was fascinated: she had just created something new and different. But she had no idea what kind of product she could make with it. Should she use her weird material to create a new type of flooring? Or maybe shape it into a piece of furniture? As she whipped up new batches and pondered how to incorporate this wood-like putty into her class project, she kept taking pinches out of her batches to fix things around the house. She used it to glue a mug back together and to reshape her sink plug so that it would fit better. She even added some to a knife handle so that she could hold it better.

The night before her project was due, ní Dhulchaointigh panicked. She had thought about all sorts of things she could make with her new material, but she hadn't yet settled on a product! And then her boyfriend at the time (now her husband) brought her into the kitchen. "Look at all of these little things you've done with your material to

> "KIDS ARE NATURAL FIXERS AND MAKERS, AND IF WE CAN GET THEM HOOKED ON THAT, WE'LL HAVE A WHOLE GENERATION OF PEOPLE WHO HAVEN'T UNLEARNED CREATIVITY—THEY'LL BE OUR NEXT GENERATION OF SOLVERS."

solve problems," he said. "What if *this* is the product? What if you aren't the designer, but everyone else is the designer?"

Ní Dhulchaointigh says this was a "penny drop" moment—it became clear that she didn't need to design a product for her class—her *material* was the product! She would call it Sugru, which comes from the word "play" in Irish.

She became so excited she filled up notebook after notebook with drawings and ideas of everything people could do with it. "How would it be useful in the garden? How would it be useful in the swimming pool? How would it be useful camping? I had this kind of imagination explosion," she says. Energized by her great idea, she experimented with her material over and over again and enlisted scientists to help her make it cleaner, smoother, and toxin-free so that even a child could handle it safely.

Finally, after five years, ní Dhulchaointigh had exactly what she was looking for: a smooth, squishy, easily moldable putty (of ingredients that are now top secret) that feels and looks like Play-Doh. It even comes in 10 different colors. Users can mold it into any shape they want, and it will harden and stick to almost any surface. It's like a cross between clay and glue.

Sugru, the world's first moldable glue, took off like a rocket. People have used it to fix everything from ripped sandals and frayed phone cords to chipped plates and broken toys. More than 15 million packs of Sugru have been sold, and it is now available in 170 countries. Ní Dhulchaointigh was named as one of Ireland's most powerful businesswomen by the Women's Executive Network and was called a "tech superhero" by CNN. And it's all because she wasn't afraid to get creative, have fun, experiment, and try something new.

Anna Stork and Andrea Sreshta

USE YOUR INGENUITY TO SOLVE
A PRESSING PROBLEM

Anna Stork and Andrea Sreshta were architecture grad students at Columbia University when a 7.0 earthquake devastated Haiti in 2010. It was a tragic disaster, killing at least 200,000 people and injuring many more. Survivors lost electricity, and some even lost their homes. Stork and Sreshta were horrified by the news and wanted to help. So, as part of a design project for school, the friends teamed up to invent something Haiti desperately needed: solar lights.

"One of the things we realized," Sreshta later said, "is that people didn't have light after dark, and it was very unsafe. People were afraid." Many people were living in tents. They needed lights to stay safe at night. And solar lights would be helpful outside of natural disasters. "Oftentimes, people in certain parts of the world have to use kerosene lanterns or candles, which are fire hazards," explained Sreshta.

While Haiti was receiving food and medical supplies from volunteers around the world, nobody was sending them lights, because lighting is heavy and expensive to ship. Plus, lights either need electricity, which Haiti didn't have, or batteries, which make shipping even more expensive. So the two women began designing a small, lightweight plastic lantern. (Newer models are as small as an iPhone and weigh only half as much.) Its small size made it inexpensive to ship—in fact, the lanterns pack flat, so 50 of them fit in the same

> ## "ANNA AND I STARTED LuminAID BECAUSE WE BELIEVE THAT LIGHT MAKES A DIFFERENCE."
>
> —ANDREA SRESHTA

box that would normally fit only eight traditional lanterns. And this lantern had many other special features. Users would blow it up like a balloon. After inflating it, they would simply press a button to turn it on. And to recharge the light, the lantern just needed some sun (no batteries, no electricity!). Stork and Sreshta also wanted their light to be waterproof so that homeless survivors could hang it outside without it getting damaged by rain.

After coming up with their design, the women needed to build it! They collected LED lights, solar panels, electronic components, and some recycled items, like inflatable products. They cut up the inflatables so they could use the valves inside them. They also collected bottle caps from sports drinks to use as caps for the valves. They then spent a few weeks building their prototype by hand in Stork's kitchen. Once they had a working lantern, they spent a few more months improving it and "testing out different components and things like that," says Stork. After many iterations, their inflatable, solar-powered prototype was complete. They decided to call their product LuminAID.

Although it was just a school project, Stork and Sreshta knew they had invented something important. After all, at the time, more than 1.1 billion people worldwide were living without electricity! LuminAID could be essential for disasters, but it could also help many towns and villages around the world that have never had electric lights. But these inspiring innovators knew their creation wouldn't help people unless they could get it out into the world. Their next step was to raise money so they could make a lot of lanterns and turn LuminAID into a real business. Their first investment came from a crowdfunding website called Indiegogo, which they used to ask the public for donations. To their delight, they received more than $50,000!

Stork and Sreshta also applied to appear on the television show *Shark Tank*, where they could present their idea to investors, who might decide to give them money to make their business happen. The young inventors couldn't have been more excited when the "sharks" invited them on the show! "We practiced a ton, thinking of every single question they could possibly ask us," said Stork. Their preparation paid off. All five "sharks" wanted to invest in LuminAID, and they ended up making a deal with one of the show's main investors, Mark Cuban. "We were really lucky to be on *Shark Tank*," Stork said, explaining that the exposure and funding from the show helped LuminAID become an international success.

While finding investors, Stork and Sreshta also partnered with a charity called ShelterBox, which buys lanterns from LuminAID and sends them to places that have been hit by disaster. Almost a decade after the bright idea was born, LuminAID, which now makes lanterns that can also charge phones, has had 100,000 lights distributed to more than 100 countries in need. And LuminAID products can be purchased by anyone. They are especially popular with backpackers and campers.

Stork credits her education for her success, explaining that in school she combined her interests of engineering, art, and architecture. "Pick and choose the courses you are most interested in, even if people say they don't fit together," she says, "because they will connect in some way, and they'll help you figure out what you want to do."

"BE AS CREATIVE AS YOU CAN WITH YOUR EDUCATION."

—ANNA STORK

Mandë Holford

FIND THE **RIGHT** MATERIALS (LIKE KILLER SNAILS AND SALAD TONGS)

When we think of snails, we usually picture cute, harmless little creatures that slowly slink across gardens. But go to a tropical climate, and you could encounter a different kind of snail: one that is shiny, colorful—and deadly. "Killer snails," as chemist Mandë Holford calls them, have venom that can kill a person in less than two hours. But Holford is finding ways that the venom can also save lives.

Holford became fascinated with killer snails after seeing a video of a snail eating a fish. She said, "I thought it was incredible, because you would think that if you put a snail and a fish in a ring, the fish would probably win. But in this case, the snail won." That's because a killer snail has a venom-filled "harpoon" that stabs toxins into its prey—mainly worms, fish, and other snails. The venom paralyzes the prey, and then the snail's mouth stretches wide open (*very* wide!) and swallows its victim.

Holford describes venom as a "cluster bomb" made from 200 to 500 components, including proteins and *peptides* (molecules that play important functions in living things). Each component can do something different, such as cause pain, paralysis, or tissue damage. Some peptides can even be converted into medicines. For instance, the peptide that paralyzes (and therefore numbs) an animal can also potentially be used as a drug to numb or take away pain in humans.

Holford, who was born in New York, started a lab in Manhattan to develop medicine from snail venom. There she discovered a peptide that "has anti-liver-cancer activity." This peptide can stop a tumor from growing. "It's the first thing we've patented," she says. "But it's not commercially available—yet." She is also working to improve a painkiller made from snail venom. Called Prialt, the drug was developed by an advisor of hers. It works well and is non-addictive, but taking it requires surgery to implant a pump inside a patient. Holford is researching a way to deliver the medicine painlessly by putting it in a microscopic "nanocontainer" that can travel through the body and pop open to release the drug when the teeny container reaches its destination (such as, perhaps, the liver). If that sounds genius, it's because it is.

Holford, who also started a game company called Killer Snails, compares science to soccer. "Science is like the soccer of careers. Everyone around the world plays soccer, because all you need is a ball," she says. "And to be a scientist, all you really need is a brain, and we're all born with brains."

HOW TO CATCH A KILLER SNAIL

As a "venomous snail hunter," Holford travels to Panama, Papua New Guinea, the Persian Gulf, Hawaii, Florida, and other tropical locations. Killer snails usually hide under sand, so, like a detective, Holford tracks them down by following their trails. Once she discovers them, she has to be careful not to get stabbed! "We don't have any anti-venom. If you're not near a hospital where they can flush you with liquid, chances are you're not going to make it," she says. So Holford, along with her team of 3 to 15 hunters (depending on the trip), makes sure to wear gloves. She also uses salad tongs to pick up each snail she collects. How does she describe her safety strategy? "It's just scuba gloves, salad tongs, and common sense," she says.

IF YOU HAVE A **CRAZY** HYPOTHESIS, TEST IT OUT!

For more than 100 years, scientists have known that the speed of light is 186,282 miles per second. They've also known they could slow light down by a tiny fraction if they shine it through water or glass. But in 1999, Danish physicist Lene Hau shocked the science world when she was able to slow light down to the speed of a bike. She then became the first person in history to actually *stop* it.

After getting her PhD in physics and becoming a teacher at Harvard University, Hau became obsessed with the coldest thing ever created on Earth—a tiny cloud of particles called a *Bose-Einstein condensate.* First made in 1995, this cloud is not a solid, liquid, or gas. It's a completely different kind of matter with very weird properties. For instance, the entire cloud, which is made up of many thousands of atoms, behaves as if it were just a single atom. What could you do with this strange matter? "I was curious to start to poke at it and see how it would react," she once said in an interview.

While poking around, an interesting *hypothesis* (a scientific hunch that needs to be tested) came to her: If the fastest thing in nature (light) shot through the coldest human-made thing in the world (a Bose-Einstein condensate cloud), would the light slow down?

She and a team of scientists and students at Harvard began to experiment. Using laser lights, they tried various colors (each of which

had a different wavelength) and beamed them into the cloud from different angles. They tried one light, and then two at the same time. In the beginning, their experiments didn't go as expected—the speed of light didn't change. For a year it was all Hau thought about. "It was so intense, I almost walked into the shower with my clothes on because we were just thinking about this all the time," she has said.

And then one day at four in the morning, she and her team finally got the formula right (the correct wavelength and angles, using two lights). At first, she shined the light into the cloud and saw a slight slowdown. Weeks later, after making adjustments, they got light to move at airplane speed and then to a much slower bicycle speed. She couldn't believe it! She had changed the speed of light from 186,282 miles per *second* to a mere 15 miles per *hour*. "Sitting there, late at night in the lab and knowing that light is going at bicycle speed and knowing that nobody in the history of mankind has been here before—that is mind-boggling," she has said. "It's worth everything." Two years later, she went further and actually stopped the light right in its tracks. Hau is the first person in history to do this.

Light is a form of energy that is visible to the human eye. When a person points a flashlight at a wall, it looks as if the wall stops the light, but it hasn't. The light has been converted to heat that people can no longer see. But in Hau's experiment, the light is trapped inside the cloud, like a prehistoric ant in a chunk of fossilized amber.

Hau made a huge scientific discovery that unlocked knowledge about how our universe works, and she continues to experiment. "We're bound to find new fundamental physics and new applications for slow light," she has said. "What exactly? It's exciting to start exploring."

"PHYSICS IS ABOUT QUESTIONING, STUDYING, PROBING NATURE."

Grace Hopper

WHEN TECHNOLOGY IS TOO COMPLEX, **HUMANIZE** IT

Grace Hopper had a knack for making really complex subjects fun and easy to grasp. For instance, when she taught math, she instructed her students to play a card game called bridge. While they played, she had them calculate the odds of different hands. They had so much fun they didn't even realize they were learning math! Hopper did the same thing for engineers, changing the highly complicated job of coding into something most engineers could understand and enjoy.

Born in 1906, Hopper was always curious about how things worked. As a young girl, she loved to take apart household gadgets to see how they were built. Once she went too far by dismantling eight alarm clocks! Her mother wasn't pleased and told her she was allowed only one alarm clock.

Hopper started her career as a math professor at Vassar College, but when the United States entered World War II in 1941, she was determined to join the Navy. At first, the Navy turned her away— they told her that, as a 100-pound, 35-year-old woman, she was too little and too old to join. But always feisty, Hopper didn't take no for an answer. She talked them into letting her join and, in 1943, she became a member of the WAVES, or Women Accepted for Voluntary Emergency Service.

Because she had a PhD in math, the Navy sent her to Harvard University as one of three coders to work on their top-secret computer calculations for war projects. The only glitch was, she didn't know how to code! But, with a sense of humor, she later explained that as part of the Navy, she had to take orders. When her boss handed her a codebook and gave her a week to learn "how to program the beast and get a program running," she did what she was told.

This was no easy task! In the early days of computers—when a computer could be bigger than a school bus, measuring 51 feet long and 8 feet high!—coding was a very specialized career. Each step was really complicated. Coders had to look in the codebook for numbers and letters that would instruct the computer to do different calculations. The instructions looked something like this: A 761 B C 7 A 761 32 B C 7. To most people, even engineers, the language looked like gibberish!

Although Hopper was able to master this language, she didn't like the fact that it was hard to learn, which kept a lot of creative people from coding. She thought there had to be an easier way to program a computer. What if coding was humanized by allowing people to program using English words? This could open the doors to a lot more coding jobs! "What I was after in beginning English language [programming]," she later said in an interview, "was to bring another whole group of people able to use the computer easily. . . . I kept calling for more user-friendly languages."

THE BUG INCIDENT

Often referred to as the "Queen of Code," Hopper is also known for her computer "bug" story. In nerd-speak, the term *bug* doesn't really have to do with live insects but means a software or programming mistake. The term had already been around, but when an actual 2-inch-long moth flew into the humongous computer Hopper was using, it broke the machine! She or someone on her team taped the squashed moth into her logbook with the caption "First actual case of bug being found." This page is now at the Smithsonian's National Museum of American History in Washington, DC.

But when she explained her idea to her bosses, they shook their heads and said it would never work. Computers wouldn't be able to read English words. She disagreed, however, and talked her colleagues into helping her move forward with her idea. Three years later, the FLOW-MATIC was born. It was the world's first programming language that accepted English word commands, instantly making programming a job that almost any computer engineer could do.

Hopper then created another easy-to-use programming language specifically for businesses. It was called Common Business Operating Language, or COBOL, which became famous worldwide and is still in use today. Her two programing languages, FLOW-MATIC and COBOL, were huge breakthroughs, and the power of coding was now available to everyone.

Hopper died of natural causes at age 85. Not only was she famous for her trailblazing work in computer programming, but she also served in the Navy for 43 years and became a rear admiral, had a ship named after her, and wrote a 500-page book explaining how to work a computer. She also predicted that computers would one day fit on a desk and be used by all kinds of people, not just programmers. But when she was asked what her greatest accomplishment was, she didn't focus on herself. She answered, "All of the young people I've trained."

> **"HUMANS ARE ALLERGIC TO CHANGE. THEY LOVE TO SAY, 'WE'VE ALWAYS DONE IT THIS WAY.' I TRY TO FIGHT THAT. THAT'S WHY I HAVE A CLOCK ON MY WALL THAT RUNS COUNTER-CLOCKWISE."**

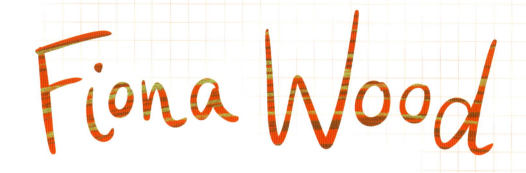

Fiona Wood

TEAM UP TO MAKE MEDICAL BREAKTHROUGHS

When someone is severely burned, they often have to get a *skin graft*, which is when a surgeon takes skin from one part of the body and transplants it to the burned area. It used to take weeks, and the long wait prolonged the patient's pain and caused horrible scarring. But plastic surgeon Fiona Wood greatly improved the lives of burn victims when she came up with an ultramodern solution: spray-on skin.

When Wood was a teenager in northern England, she trained to be an Olympic sprinter, but that dream didn't happen. "I wasn't good enough," she says with a laugh. "I was a better academic than I was a runner." So she took what she learned from athletics—doing something she loved and working hard—and applied it to medical school. One day in college, she saw a four-year-old boy with a terrible scar from spilled hot coffee. Not only did the boy have a bad permanent scar, but he also suffered from itchiness and pain. "You've got to be able to do something *more* about this," Wood thought, and she decided to specialize in plastic surgery to help burn victims. In the 1980s, she moved abroad and, in 1991, became the very first woman plastic surgeon in Western Australia.

To replace skin, doctors have traditionally shaved a bit of healthy skin from a burn patient's body and used the cells from the sample to grow sheets of skin in a box. This is the part that took about three weeks in a lab. The new sheets of skin were usually fragile and difficult to transplant. While waiting, the patient developed disfiguring scars and was at risk of infection. Wood was determined to find a way to replace large areas of burned skin faster, without all the pain and scarring.

She partnered with scientist Marie Stoner to research the problem. After a lot of observation, they noticed something interesting. Samples of cells, which are kind of like a soup before they grow into sheets, "are much stickier—they stick to the wounds better" than the sheets do, Wood later said. And this made them wonder if they could grow the cells right on the body, rather than first growing them in a box. This would allow patients to receive new skin cells right away, without all of the scarring they would get while waiting for a transplant.

> "SOMEONE ASKED ME THE OTHER DAY, 'WHAT'S IT LIKE AT THE TOP?' AND I THOUGHT, 'WHERE'S THE TOP?'"

This seemed like a great idea! But the scientists weren't sure how to apply the cell goop to the burn wounds. Should they dip the burned skin into a container of the "soupy" cells or pour the cells onto the burns? Or maybe wrap the burns with cell-soaked bandages? "Our ideas were sparking," she says. "And then one of us—we don't remember who—said, 'What if we just spray them on?'" It was an offhand remark, but suddenly the women looked at each other and thought, "Whoa!"

They scrambled to figure out if there was a spray that would keep the cells alive and undamaged. They went to the pharmacy and gathered all kinds of spray products—nose sprays, throat sprays, hair sprays, numbing sprays—and "tested a whole lot of nozzle systems until we found the one that was perfect," Wood says. And that turned out to be an Italian mouth freshener spray. After 20 years, "it's still the one we use."

In 1999, Wood and Stoner's spray-on skin, which they called ReCell, was ready for the world. But, at first, the world seemed hesitant to embrace the futuristic treatment. It wasn't until 2002, when two bombs exploded in Bali, Indonesia, that Wood was able to prove how significant her invention was. Twenty-eight of the most seriously wounded survivors were flown to her hospital. Wood, who was in charge of the burn unit, felt a tremendous responsibility to save all these lives. At first, this made her feel alone. But then she took a moment and noticed the 19 surgeons and 130 other medical workers around her, all pitching in, working around the clock to do their part. She wasn't alone—she was part of a team. "The power of people coming together, it was extraordinary," she says. In the end, 25 of her patients survived, which was incredible, considering the devastating condition they had been in.

In 2005, Wood was named Australian of the Year, and her spray-on skin technology is now used in hospitals around the world. Wood credits her success to "all of the amazing people who helped us along the way." She had faced many challenges, which she compares to the colorful squares on a Rubik's Cube. In order to solve "a complex puzzle," she says, "the solution is people." To line everything up, she believes, you need teamwork. "One thing I learned was that it's not weakness to ask for help."

Raye Montague

DON'T LET **OBSTACLES** DISCOURAGE YOU

When Raye Montague was seven years old in Arkansas, during World War II, she and her grandpa climbed down a ladder to see a traveling attraction: a captured German submarine. "It was like a tin can," she later said. She got to look through the periscope, and she was excited by "all of the dials and mechanisms" in the sub. She asked a man in charge, "What do you have to know to do this?" His reply? "Oh, you'd have to be an engineer, but you don't ever have to worry about that." What he meant was that since she was a black girl, she would never have the opportunity to become an engineer. His words were insulting, but she didn't pay him any mind. Instead, she decided to find out what she needed to do to become an engineer.

It was true that she faced obstacles. "You're female, you're black, and you'll have a Southern segregated school education," her mother pointed out. "But you can be or do anything you want, provided you're educated." Montague took her mother's advice to heart. Since she wasn't allowed to study engineering, she got a degree in business. Still, she was determined to become an engineer!

After graduating from college in 1956, she got a job with the Navy as an office clerk. It had nothing to do with engineering. So she asked an engineer if he could teach her how to use a computer. "No!" the man said, "the next thing you'll want is my job!" His refusal to help was an obstacle, but Montague found a way around it. She had a photographic memory, so she learned how to use the computer by looking over his shoulder and watching him work. "Two weeks later, all the engineers called in sick," she later said. She went to her coworker's computer and started doing his job. When the boss walked in and saw how well she was doing, he gave the job to her.

At one point, part of Montague's new job was teaching some of the guys how to use a computer, and she found out that even though she knew more than they did, their salaries were higher than hers. She asked for a raise, but her boss said no. He told her that with the raise, she would have to work the night shift. He knew she didn't have a car, and there was no public transportation at night. He thought that excuse would shut her up.

But it didn't.

Montague immediately bought a car and taught herself how to drive. She started driving to work even before she had a license! Surprised, her boss gave her the raise.

In the early 1970s, after years of hard work, she ended up with a boss who didn't like her. "He had a problem with me," she later said. "I hate to say this, but he was a racist. So he decided . . . to get rid of me." His plan was to give her an impossible task. That way, when she failed, he could fire her. He asked her to create a computer program that engineers could use to design a ship. He gave her six months

"I'VE HAD TO FIGHT EVERY STEP OF THE WAY AND CREATE EVERY JOB I'VE HAD."

to complete it. What he didn't tell her was that the Navy had been trying to create this program for six years without success. The other engineers couldn't get the correct text and layout to work.

Never one to say no, Montague agreed. She came in after work hours because she "had to tear the system apart and reassemble it," she said. She opened up the printer and inserted an IBM device called a "TN print chain," which allowed text to print out in the way the Navy needed (with both uppercase and lowercase letters, printed in two columns). In six months, she presented her supervisor at the Navy with their first successful computer program to design ships. Though she'd tackled a seemingly unbeatable task, her supervisor had no plans to use her impressive work.

But when President Richard Nixon heard what she had done, he asked if Montague could actually use her computer program to design a real ship. This had never been done before. Ships had only been drafted by hand, and it took around two years to design each ship. But the president wanted ships right away. In fact, he asked, could she design a ship in only *two months*? As if by magic, she did what he asked—in 18 hours and 26 minutes! She became the first person in history to design a ship using a computer—with a program she had gotten to work.

TURN OBSTACLES INTO CHALLENGES

Montague, whose ship designs are still being used, once said, "An obstacle is when they say you can't or you're wrong." Her advice was to think of *obstacles* as *challenging situations*. She says by feeling challenged—and working hard—she was able to smash right through any obstacles and reach the top of her field. "And you can do the same thing."

Sha Yao

CREATE OBJECTS **WITH BEAUTY AND FUNCTION** IN MIND

Product designers are people who create everyday objects like plates, brooms, tables, iPhone cases, and cars. Some designers care more about how stylish the object is, while other designers care more about how well it works. Sha Yao focuses on both, and in her twenties, she created beautiful bowls, cups, and utensils that also have a very important function: helping people with Alzheimer's eat.

Yao grew up in Taipei, where she was close to her grandmother. She loved to draw and design new things. She especially enjoyed designing bamboo lanterns, and in elementary school, she even entered them in design competitions for kids. So when Yao was accepted to graduate school at the Academy of Art University in San Francisco, she was excited. She couldn't wait to learn how to design real products! But she was also sad to leave her grandmother, who had recently been diagnosed with *Alzheimer's*, a disease that causes memory loss and typically affects people 65 and older.

Yao's grandmother had become very forgetful and was having trouble at mealtime. "She forgot how to eat with proper kitchen utensils, and she would even forget to eat," says Yao. "Food would drop everywhere, and she would tip cups often." So as she was getting ready to leave for college in the United States, Yao decided she wanted to invent a product for her school project that would help her grandmother eat. She approached this project as both a scientist and a designer. Before she knew exactly what she would design, she needed to do research to figure out what the biggest eating challenges were for people with Alzheimer's. So she volunteered at a senior care facility. She also did research online.

Through her research, she found many ways to improve the design of tableware for people like her grandmother. For example, designing bowls and cups with bright colors adds contrast so people can see the food better, while adding some weight and rubber bottoms to cups keeps them from easily tipping over or sliding away. To make it easier to spoon up food, Yao added a slant to her bowls so the food would gravitate toward one spot. She gave a special curve to the spoons and created a right-angle edge (like a wall) on one side of the bowl to help with scooping. These were other innovations that made it easier for Alzheimer's patients to scoop up food.

By combining math with design, Yao created a bright and useful nine-piece tableware set called Eatwell, which looks like it belongs in a fashion magazine. She then entered it in the 2014 Stanford Center on Longevity Design Challenge and won first place! This award helped push Eatwell into the public eye. "The recognition from winning— and even just participating in—the challenge helped to inspire new investors as well as users," she says. "The challenge really gave us a lot of exposure. It was like winning a lottery." But a lottery is won

"IT'S REALLY IMPORTANT TO KNOW WHAT YOU WANT TO DO, AND THEN DO IT."

by sheer luck, while Eatwell came in first place because of Yao's ingenuity, talent, and imagination.

Yao says caregivers from across the United States and from all over the world have given her very positive feedback. Although Eatwell, which was on the list of *Time* magazine's "25 Best Inventions of 2016," was invented with Alzheimer's in mind, it has turned out to be helpful for people with all kinds of physical challenges, such as those with Parkinson's, a disease that affects movement control in some older people.

And now, even though her grandmother died a few years before she created Eatwell, Yao continues to work on new products to further help others with Alzheimer's, such as one that will prevent them from getting lost and wandering away from home. She is looking at products that already exist, "but each product has problems," she says. For example, a bracelet with a GPS tracker needs batteries ("How can you assume they will remember to charge their devices?"), and some trackers don't work well in all locations. "I want to improve the experience and see what I can do to come up with better solutions."

Yao, who has lived in California for more than 10 years, believes that anyone with a good product idea can make it happen, but the important thing is not to give up. "Most people have great ideas, but for one reason or another they think, 'Oh no! It might not work.' So they stop," she says. "Good ideas don't grow by themselves. You have to just keep going. Don't stop."

Martine Rothblatt

DON'T BE AFRAID TO CHASE "IMPOSSIBLE" IDEAS

In the early 1990s, Martine Rothblatt got some news that no parent wants to hear: her eight-year-old daughter, Jenesis, was dying. The young girl, who was short of breath and fainting a lot, was diagnosed with pulmonary arterial hypertension (PAH), a fatal lung disease. Jenesis would probably not live past the age of 13. But Rothblatt, who wasn't a doctor, didn't accept what the experts told her. Instead, she quit her high-paying job in satellite radio to try and invent a new drug to save her daughter's life.

PAH is very rare, and the doctors told her that her plan was impossible. How could someone without any medical experience invent a life-saving treatment? But Rothblatt, a trans woman who grew up in San Diego, California, was determined to save her daughter. She would prove these doctors wrong. She began by reading everything she could about biology, a subject she hadn't studied since 10th grade.

This wasn't the first time Rothblatt had ignored the "experts" to accomplish the impossible. Years earlier, as someone who had always loved space science, she had an incredible realization while visiting a NASA satellite installation in the Seychelles islands: "When I saw that a handheld antenna could receive a GPS signal from space, I thought, 'Why not also a radio signal from space?'"

The whole world could be connected by satellite radio!

Satellite radio gives listeners hundreds of stations, rather than just a few dozen. People can tune in to their favorite programs—without any static—anywhere in the country. (With regular radio, stations are local and disappear when you drive too far away.) If you live in California but want to hear a jazz show in New York, satellite radio makes it possible.

Everybody, including the FCC (Federal Communications Commission, part of the US government), told Rothblatt that satellite radio wouldn't work. There were too many technological, as well as legal, obstacles. But she was an attorney who specialized in space law, and she did not take no for an answer. She made all kinds of calculations and demonstrations, proved it was indeed possible, and in 1990, founded and became the chief executive officer (CEO) of Sirius Satellite Radio, which later became Sirius XM.

This is the job she left behind when Jenesis was diagnosed. In fact, she put the rest of her life on hold and focused only on finding a cure for PAH. One day, while sitting in a hospital library doing research, Rothblatt came across an old publication that changed everything. It described a drug for another illness that had a particular side effect, and Rothblatt realized that this side effect was something that would help treat her daughter's symptoms! She immediately started researching the drug. She then convinced a

INNOVATIONS ON THE HORIZON

Rothblatt is currently working on two other "impossible" projects, both of which seem like science fiction but are real. The first involves donated lungs that sit in a glass incubator at UT's new division, Lung Biotechnology. Using technology that Rothblatt helped pioneer, the lungs are repaired and then transplanted into people who need them. With a national shortage of transplantable lungs, Rothblatt is constantly researching new ways to make more lungs available.

Her second major project is developing the first electric helicopter, which experts also reacted to with a big no! They said it could not be done because batteries were too heavy. But she ignored them, and her team has already flown their electric helicopter prototypes!

hesitant pharmacologist to work with her, and she quickly launched a medical foundation called United Therapeutics (UT). Within a few years, Rothblatt perfected new drugs—including one called Orenitram (Martine Ro spelled backward)—that were approved by the FDA (Food and Drug Administration). The drugs were groundbreaking, and they saved tens of thousands of people from PAH. Jenesis got her life back and is now in her thirties, living an active, healthy life.

Creating lifesaving drugs—not to mention Sirius XM—is already more than what most people do in a lifetime, but Rothblatt didn't stop there. In fact, the list of Rothblatt's medical inventions keeps growing. Along with one drug came an under-the-skin pump. "I had to make not only the medicine, but also a way to deliver it continuously," she says. "This is because the medicine only lasts 30 minutes inside the body, but patients require it to be active 24 hours a day to stay healthy. So I had to invent a special kind of pump to pump the medicine through a patient's skin 24/7."

There seems to be no end to what Rothblatt can dream up and accomplish, from creating medicine to satellite radio to electric helicopters. But she doesn't think of herself as a superhero. "Almost all inventions and discoveries are made by common people who just do uncommon things," she says. "Everyone reading this book has the ability to make a difference with a big idea in space or medicine. Most important is not to give up."

"THERE ARE MILLIONS OF THINGS TO DISCOVER ABOUT MEDICINE AND SPACE. OUT OF ALL THOSE THINGS, SURELY EACH AND EVERY ONE OF US CAN MAKE A BIG DIFFERENCE."

electric

Ada Lovelace

PUT YOUR IMAGINATION TO THE TEST

In 1828, when Ada Lovelace was 12 years old, she wanted to fly. So she got out her pens and paper and began mapping out plans for how she could make this happen. She drew wings based on her observation of birds, and she thought about what kind of materials to use (paper, silk, wires, feathers). She calculated measurements and wrote instructions. She even created a booklet called *Flyology*, which explained her ideas and included beautiful illustrations she drew herself.

It's common for imaginative children to dream up inventions, but what made Lovelace's project so astonishing was the amount of research, time, and detail she put into her flying machine. She even had a list of what to bring on her flight, including a map and compass to help her "cut across the country by the most direct road." And this was more than 75 years before the Wright brothers made their first successful flight in an airplane!

Amazingly, her steam-powered flying machine wasn't the only invention from the future she dreamed up. Lovelace also predicted the modern computer and became the world's first computer programmer—even though computers as we know them wouldn't be around until the next century.

Born Augusta Ada Byron, Ada was from a wealthy family in England. Her mother left her father, the famous poet Lord Byron, and took her away when she was an infant. When Lovelace was only four years old, her mother hired governesses to teach her math and science so she wouldn't become a poet like her father.

As a child, Lovelace suffered from an illness that left her with terrible headaches. Soon after that, she came down with a horrible case of measles that left her temporarily paralyzed. She was forced to lie in bed for more than a year. Of course, these were the days before TV and YouTube, so her mother surrounded her with tutors and governesses who kept her busy learning. Math and science, considered "masculine subjects" in the 1800s, were always included.

Lovelace's interest in math magnified after meeting an inventor at age 17. She was at a party when the host, Charles Babbage, told her about a "computer" called the Difference Engine he had created that could calculate numbers. She was captivated, and the two quickly became friends. He was impressed with her sharp mind and called her the "Enchantress of Number."

A few years later, she married William King, who would become the Earl of Lovelace (making her a countess!). They had three children. But she didn't let domestic life stop her from working with Babbage on his second calculating machine, called the Analytical Engine.

While translating a French article about Babbage's second "Engine" into English, she spent almost a year adding her own notes,

"MATHEMATICAL SCIENCE SHOWS US WHAT IS. IT IS THE LANGUAGE OF UNSEEN RELATIONS BETWEEN THINGS."

which were nearly three times the length of the original paper. In one section, she detailed how computers would be able to do more than just calculate numbers—they would also be able to use numbers as symbols to create music, graphics, and maybe even allow the computer to think for itself (which we now call *artificial intelligence*).

She also wrote an *algorithm* (a list of steps that help people solve mathematical problems) for the Analytical Engine that would compute *Bernoulli numbers*, which are a sequence of numbers that help people study whole number mathematics. It was basically the same algorithm that computers would later use, and it is now considered by many experts to be the first computer program ever written!

Lovelace, also known as Lady Lovelace, was proud of her work and knew that she had created something important. "This is a pleasant prospect for the future," she said, "as I suppose many hundreds and thousands of such formulae will come forth from my pen, in one way or another."

Although she never lived to see her brilliant ideas become reality, her name hasn't been forgotten. In her honor, the US Department of Defense named a programming language "Ada." Ada College was created in London for technology students, and Ada Lovelace Day is observed every October to celebrate women in technology. She was someone who combined imagination with intellect to predict the future and is now recognized by the world as a visionary.

Sandra Pascoe Ortiz

EXPERIMENT WITH **NEW MATERIALS** TO RID THE WORLD OF PLASTIC

Humans have a plastic problem. With more than eight billion tons of plastic tossed into the ocean every year, plastic is destroying ocean life. Sea animals suffocate in plastic bags or eat them, which is toxic. Then seafood becomes toxic to humans. But what if plastic wasn't harmful? What if it quickly disappeared after soaking in water? Fortunately, there is such a plastic in the works, thanks to a resourceful chemical engineer named Sandra Pascoe Ortiz—and cactus slime.

Professor Ortiz, whose university lab is in western Mexico, started experimenting with cacti after some of her chemistry students asked if she could help them make earth-friendly plastic for a science fair. When the semester ended, the students gave up. But Ortiz thought it was too good an idea to let go. "This can be done!" she thought. So she continued to experiment, along with a new group of students. She uses a blender to spin cactus into plastic. And unlike traditional plastic, which can take up to a thousand years to decompose, her plastic disintegrates in two weeks if it is sitting in water.

It took a lot of trial and error for Ortiz and her team to come up with a prototype. Working tirelessly, she collected prickly pear cacti (*nopales* in Spanish), which grow wild all over Mexico. She figured the cactus plant would make a great base for plastic, since it contains a sugary interior that is *viscous*—thick, sticky, and goopy. Experiment after experiment, she juiced the cactus in a blender, creating a very gummy slime. She then strained and refrigerated the goo. Once it was chilled, she tried many variations of a recipe that included mixing the slime with wax, different kinds of proteins, and natural colors. After mixing, she thinly spread it over hot plates to dry.

After five years, she has come up with a plastic that is ready for the world. (The patent is pending.) "We can obtain different colors, shapes, thicknesses," she has said. "We can make plastics that are very smooth or very flexible, and we can make others that are more rigid." Even more importantly, she has explained, "It's a nontoxic product. All the materials we use can be ingested both by humans or animals, and they won't cause any harm."

It takes 10 days to make the plastic, but with industrial machines, she thinks the process will be a lot faster. Ortiz is now working to "make a sustainable business plan to cultivate the raw materials without endangering the environment," she says. Since cacti stay alive and keep growing leaves after some have been cut off, her plan should work. She thinks her plastic will make great shopping bags, costume jewelry, and toys, for starters. "The whole project has been a challenge. It has been a long journey of learning, and of success and errors, that has allowed us to reach this point," she says. Ortiz credits curiosity and perseverance to her success. "Never stop pursuing your dreams. Read a lot and prepare yourself, because the world needs more scientists to help make it better."

"THE PROJECT ARISES FROM AN ECOLOGICAL CONCERN TO TRY TO REPLACE . . . THE PLASTICS DERIVED FROM OIL."

Doris Sung

DESIGN BUILDINGS THAT CAN CHANGE THE WORLD

Doris Sung isn't an ordinary architect. Many of her creations seem more like living creatures than stationary structures. They breathe, move, and sometimes even appear to have personalities. These buildings and installations seem magical because of a skin-like *smart material* (a material that reacts to things) she developed. This material allows buildings to cool down—and warm back up—on their own, without using a speck of electricity.

To get an idea of how her "building skin" works, look at human skin. Human skin is like a thermostat that helps control people's body temperature. When people are hot, their skin sweats to cool down their body. When they are chilled, their skin shrinks its pores to warm up their body. Now imagine if buildings also had skin that reacted to temperature. This is exactly what Sung is creating!

It all started when Sung, a professor at the University of Southern California (USC), was exploring ways to make buildings more planet-friendly. She stumbled across a material called *thermobimetal* (a type of sheet metal that curls up when it's heated). This material was a game-changer for Sung. "When I first got a sample of thermobimetal from the manufacturer, I felt like a kid. I just had to go outside and put it in the sun and watch it curl over and over," she later said. "I could not believe there was no energy required." And she had an

incredible idea. What if she used it as a building cover to replace materials like bricks, glass, and wood?

Sung experimented. She cut up sheet after sheet of thermobimetal. She tried out different shapes, heating each one to see how it responded. After cutting thousands of pieces and connecting them all together, she created a "building skin" that looked a bit like fish scales. "There's always a moment where things start working, and it's an exhilarating moment," she says.

When hit by the sun, the silver shapes lift on their own, each at a different angle depending on their location from the sun, to create a good "sun-shading device" for a building. Cut differently, the pieces of thermobimetal can curl to allow airflow into and out of the building, like a vent. In cold weather, the pieces flatten into their original shape.

Sung realizes this material could have a huge impact on architecture—and on the environment. But being the first person to introduce sustainable architecture in this way hasn't been easy. "There are zero role models for me," she says. "Not having anyone go before you is, I guess, both a good and bad thing." She says it's mostly good, because everything she does is so groundbreaking.

But being a trailblazer can be hard, because something so novel takes time for people to accept. "People are resistant to change when it comes to building." So Sung must be patient. She tells future innovators to make noise. "It's really important to speak up, talk loudly, ask questions, and ultimately be curious."

> **"WE HAVE TO RETHINK THE WAY WE BUILD, AND WHAT WE BUILD WITH. IF WE DON'T, OUR PROBLEMS WILL ONLY GET WORSE."**

Valerie L. Thomas

IF YOU AREN'T SURE HOW SOMETHING WORKS, FIGURE IT OUT

Imagine being a surgeon in the operating room who can see a patient's heart in 3-D, floating in the air in front of you. And you don't even need to wear 3-D glasses! This type of image is possible because of something called an *illusion transmitter*, a technology invented by NASA scientist Valerie L. Thomas after she watched an optical trick involving a light bulb.

As a child in Maryland in the 1950s, nobody ever encouraged Thomas to learn science. She became fascinated by electronics after watching her father fix the television. At about seven years old, she visited the library and brought home *The Boys First Book on Electronics*, which was filled with projects. Although her father was excited about the book, "he didn't think about doing it with me," she says. Thomas was a girl, and she was expected to do "girl things," like sewing. She returned the book to the library without trying any of its activities.

Her middle school and high school didn't offer courses in electronics. "However, we had physics in high school, so I took a class in physics," she says. Later, she ended up being one of only two women in her class at Morgan State University to get a degree in physics. Her degree and her love of math and science landed her a lifelong career at NASA.

While she was manager of Landsat (a NASA program that has been taking satellite images of Earth's surface since 1972 to see how it changes over time), she went to a science exhibition where she saw a demonstration that changed her life. "From a distance, I saw a plain lamp on the table, and on top of the lamp was a light bulb," she recalls. "The person turned the light bulb on, and then unscrewed the light bulb and took it out of the lamp." Thomas saw the light bulb taken away, but it looked like the light bulb was still in the lamp, all lit up! "That caught my attention," she says. "I knew my brain saw it being taken out, but my eyes saw that it was still there. I went to the table to touch the light bulb, and my finger went right through it."

Thomas was astonished. She headed straight to the physics section of the library and looked for books about optics. There she found examples of *virtual images* and *real images,* which she remembered learning about in college. When people look into a flat mirror, they see what is known in optics as a virtual image that looks like it is inside or behind the glass. Real images, on the other hand, are 3-D images (not on a screen but right before you, as if they are real). She realized that the illusion she saw at the exhibition was created with a *concave mirror* (a curved mirror shaped like the inside of a bowl). By positioning an object in front of a concave mirror, a realistic 3-D image of the object is formed *in front of* (and at a distance from) the mirror. She imagined a setup made up of *two* concave mirrors that would send hologram-like images to another location. "And that's how I came up with the 'illusion transmitter,'" she says.

"GRADES ARE IMPORTANT, BUT IT'S THE LEARNING THAT REALLY MATTERS."

The illusion transmitter works like this: A camera takes video of the first concave mirror, which has an object (say, an apple) in front of it. The video's image is then sent (like a livestream) to a video projector that is sitting somewhere else, where it is aimed at the second concave mirror. Anyone looking toward the second mirror will see a live 3-D image of the apple in front of it, as if it's really there. So cool!

Thomas researched and developed her invention with the help of a four-year-old assistant—her son. As a parent, she believed in exposing her child to science at a (very!) young age. "He helped me when I was setting up, looking for my images that were displayed in the air," she says. "At one point I was trying to see how far I could project the image in the air, and I couldn't find it. Then I heard this little voice. 'Mommy, mommy, here it is!'" In 1978, Thomas applied for a patent for her illusion transmitter. She received it two years later. Since then, NASA has used her technology, and scientists have worked on ways to use the illusion transmitter for surgery and television technology.

Thomas retired from NASA in 1995. She now volunteers with STEM education outreach organizations, helping kids do cool things like fly real airplanes and build telescopes. She wants them to have opportunities that she didn't have as a child. For girls interested in STEM, Thomas says, "Don't let the boys dictate who you are or what you're supposed to do. Have confidence and just do it."

Build your own TELESCOPE

manila frame

lens

manila frame

large mailing tube

eyepiece

Sarah Parcak

LEARN TO SEE THINGS
DIFFERENTLY

When Sarah Parcak was young, she loved hunting for sand dollars on the beach near her home in Maine. At first, it was difficult to spot the flat, white treasures against the sand, but she learned to recognize their patterns and shapes, and then collecting them became easy. She soon developed a "passion for finding things." Little did she know that this passion would lead her to find Itjtawy, an ancient Egyptian city that had been missing for 4,000 years. And she found it not by searching on the ground, but by taking photos from space!

Of course the perfect job for someone who likes to find things is being an *archaeologist*, a scientist who digs in the earth to find ancient objects and cities and helps people understand past civilizations. But knowing where to dig can be tricky. Earth is a huge planet, and it can take years to locate an area where objects from the distant past are buried. But Parcak uses high-tech methods, which makes finding locations to dig a lot easier. She starts her process with *satellite imagery* (images of Earth captured by satellites up in space). "When I started studying Egyptology, I realized that seeing with my naked eyes alone wasn't enough," she said in a TED Talk. "This is what brought me to using satellite imagery. For trying to map the past, I knew I had to see differently."

Archaeologists (or *space* archaeologists, as Parcak says) were already using satellite images to help them zero in on locations, but these images showed only what was on Earth's surface, and Parcak wanted to see what was underneath. So she figured out a way to see the images differently by exposing them to infrared light. Infrared can detect different chemicals under Earth's surface, so if there is a buried ancient clay house, its chemicals will show up as a bright color that stands out against the rest of the image. This has completely transformed the way archaeologists find their digs.

Because of her new technique using infrared, Parcak has been able to locate 1,000 lost tombs, 3,100 lost settlements, and possibly 17 previously unknown pyramids in places like Romania, Italy, Scotland, Iceland, Peru, and, of course, Egypt. And, like Indiana Jones, she even revealed the layout of Egypt's *actual* lost city of Tanis (the city they were looking for in the movie *Raiders of the Lost Ark*!).

But Parcak's biggest—and favorite—discovery was locating the important city of Itjtawy (pronounced itch-TAO-wee), the capital of Egypt during the time period known as the Middle Kingdom (approximately 2030 BC–1650 BC). Although Egyptians and archaeologists knew the general area where Itjtawy might be, it was extremely difficult to find (which is why it was lost for 4,000 years). "How do you find a buried city in a vast landscape?" she asked at

JOIN AN ONLINE SCIENCE EXPEDITION

How would you like to hunt for excavation sites that might have buried objects and cities? Parcak recently launched an online app that invites everyone (including you!) to help discover new digs. After receiving the $1 million TED Prize in 2016, she used the money to launch GlobalXplorer°, a "citizen science platform," which means people across the globe can work together as scientists to accomplish a goal—or "virtual expedition" in this case. Once you sign up, you get access to satellite imagery for a specific country, along with images, or "tiles," which you can examine for any signs of a buried past. So far, the expeditions have been in Peru and India, and ordinary people have helped discover 324 potential sites in Peru alone!

TED 2012. "Finding it randomly would be the equivalent of locating a needle in a haystack—blindfolded, wearing baseball mitts," she explained.

But Parcak had a strong suspicion she'd located the ancient capital when a huge swath of land showed up on her manipulated satellite images as neon pink. In 2015, she and her team, along with a team of Egyptian scientists, investigated. At first, they found pottery under thick mud in the area about 16 feet under the earth. They then found stones, like amethyst, agate, and quartz, which were valued and worn as jewelry during the Middle Kingdom. Since then, Parcak has been working with Egypt's Ministry of Antiquities as the co-director of this site, uncovering pyramids, tombs, and a rich history about the buried capital. "It's a really special place," she says.

Although Parcak enjoys the detective work of figuring out where buried sites are through satellite images, she enjoys excavating even more. "Both are really fun, but the digging is what I live for," she says.

"I want kids and teens to know we are in a golden age of archaeological discovery," Parcak says. For anyone who wants to be an archaeologist, she suggests studying all kinds of science, including archaeology, physics, chemistry, and computer science. "We won't run out of things to find anytime soon, and we'll need lots of great science to help us map and explore them."

> **"EGYPT JUST GRABBED ME WHEN I WAS SMALL. IT CALLED TO ME. IT STILL DOES, EVERY DAY."**

Stephanie Kwolek

LISTEN TO YOUR GUT

Kevlar is a plastic material that seems magical. It's five times stronger than steel, flexible enough to cushion sneakers, and so heat resistant it protects people from getting burned. It's used to make everything from skis to oven mitts to body armor. But in 1965, when chemist Stephanie Kwolek first invented its mysterious fibers in her lab, others said it was junk to be tossed in the trash. She had to convince them that it was special.

Kwolek started working as a chemist for DuPont, a chemical company, when she was 23 years old. They didn't usually hire women to work as scientists, but this was in the 1940s, when many men had left the United States to fight in World War II, giving women more job opportunities. After 18 years at the company, DuPont gave Kwolek a challenge: Could she create a lightweight and super-strong fiber to replace the steel reinforcements used in car tires?

"The assignment that I had been given was something that nobody else wanted to do," she once said in an interview. Her colleagues were too busy with other projects. But she really enjoyed research, especially with *polymers* (long chains of molecules), which is what rubber and plastics are made of. Kwolek spent months and months experimenting with different polymer solutions, trying to create a fiber that was light yet strong enough to hold up the weight of a tire.

Experimenting with chemicals wasn't Kwolek's dream job when she was growing up in Pennsylvania in the 1920s. As a girl, she loved sewing and working with fabrics. She would sketch for hours, hoping to become a fashion designer one day. But her mother, who was a seamstress, discouraged her, saying she was too much of a perfectionist and would become too frustrated designing clothes. So Kwolek, who was also interested in science, got a college degree in chemistry. Although she wouldn't be designing clothes, she'd have a chance to work with molecules to design new materials.

DuPont had made other plastics with polymer solutions that were clear, thick, and goopy, so these were the qualities that Kwolek looked for in her experiments. But one day, after months of trying

"A LOT OF DISCOVERIES ARE PURELY ACCIDENTAL."

different solutions, she created a batch at a lower temperature than usual. This batch turned into a solution unlike any other: instead of thick and clear, it was thin and foggy, the color of a pearl. She placed some of this strange solution on a spatula and, instead of the honeylike way these mixtures usually flowed off the utensil, this one ran off the spatula like water. Yet it was as sticky as glue. This strange concoction turned out to be a *liquid crystalline* solution, meaning it is something that is in between being a liquid and a solid. Kwolek was curious.

"It was unlike any of the polymer solutions that we had," she said. "It was cloudy, and you thought, 'Well this is one of the no-no's.'" She had assumed the cloudy appearance meant the solution contained unwanted solid particles. But something told her to investigate further, so she ran it through a fine filter, and surprisingly, the color remained the same. She then asked a technician at the lab if he would try spinning it into fiber by putting it into a *spinneret*, a machine that separates denser liquids from lighter liquids. But the technician refused! He thought she was wrong and that the murky solution had solid particles in it that would clog up his machine.

But listening to her gut, Kwolek persisted. For weeks she "tortured" him, as she later joked, until he finally gave in and spun her mystery material in the spinneret, just to stop her from asking him again. "It spun beautifully," she later said.

She now had new fibers, which she sent to a testing lab to determine their strength. When she received the results, she was shocked. "When I got the numbers back, I was rather skeptical," she later recalled. "I thought maybe they'd made a mistake." So she retested the fibers over and over, and sure enough, the new material was stronger than anyone had imagined it would be. Although its chemical name is poly-paraphenylene terephthalamide, DuPont named it Kevlar, a much easier name to pronounce!

By the mid-1970s, Kevlar became a huge success. Besides car tires, the super-strong material is best known for its use in bulletproof vests, which have saved thousands of lives. It is also used in boats, tennis rackets, gloves, jackets, athletic shoes, Ping-Pong paddles, cell phones, and hundreds of other products. "I never in a thousand years expected that little liquid crystal to develop into what it did," Kwolek once said.

Kevlar has made billions of dollars for DuPont. But Kwolek never personally made a profit from her invention, since she created it for DuPont. She did, however, become famous around the world. In 1995, she was inducted into the National Inventors Hall of Fame, and she got to meet many well-known people, including President Bill Clinton. She worked at DuPont for 40 years, and after she retired in her sixties, she continued to advise them when they asked. She died in 2014 at age 90.

Chieko Asakawa

TURN YOUR CHALLENGES INTO STRENGTHS

Born in Osaka, Japan, Chieko Asakawa was an active girl who played sports. Unlike many young people who grew up to become inventors, she wasn't interested in technology. She dreamed of becoming an Olympic athlete. But her dream was shattered at age 11, when she accidentally hit her left eye against the side of a swimming pool, damaging her vision. By the age of 14, she was completely blind. Although the accident was devastating, it led her to become a brilliant inventor who found clever ways to help others.

After losing her sight, life became more difficult. She had to rely on others for help with almost everything. For instance, reading schoolbooks was impossible. So she spent painstaking hours transcribing her books into Braille with a special Braille "typewriter." But in order to do that, she needed her brothers to read the books to her. Understandably, her brothers were not always in the mood, and sometimes they hid from her! She wished she could be more independent. But how could she be more independent without her sight? Technology, she soon realized, was the answer.

In the early 1980s, computer technology was advancing at a rapid pace, making most people's lives easier. But technology was ignoring the needs of people who were blind or visually impaired. "In those days, the method to create Braille was very, very low tech," she says, referring to the way she had to manually transcribe her books. She wondered why computers weren't creating books in Braille. "That's the moment my innovation journey began," she said in a presentation at a TED event.

Asakawa went to school to become a computer engineer and, in 1985, she got a job as a researcher at the computer company IBM in Tokyo. Within one year of working there, she asked IBM if she could focus on *assistive technology* (technology that helps people with disabilities do things). IBM said yes, and in a short time, Asakawa developed a word processor that allowed users to write and edit in Braille using an ordinary computer keyboard. She also created a Braille library network that made it easier to share Braille books and determine which books were already transcribed into Braille. Her creations offered visually impaired people in Japan an endless source of books that had once been difficult to access.

But it was Asakawa's 1997 invention—the IBM Home Page Reader—that made her a star. The Home Page Reader was a system that turned text from the Internet into speech, so people could hear anything that was on the Web. This technology has completely changed the lives of millions of blind and visually impaired people worldwide, who now have the same access to news, sports, online shopping, and any kind of information imaginable as everyone else does. This was such a revolutionary innovation that, in May 2019, Asakawa was inducted into the US National Inventors Hall of Fame.

A ROBOTIC SUITCASE

One of Asakawa's favorite projects is her "AI suitcase" robot that can roll around on its own. The suitcase, which will fit a laptop and maybe one day's worth of clothing, helps blind people in airports by steering them and giving them updated flight information. It also warns them when there are stairs or other obstacles they need to navigate. Asakawa loves to travel and looks forward to the autonomy the robotic suitcase will give her and other visually impaired people once it's available to the public.

Asakawa, who now lives in the United States, is currently developing technology that goes beyond books and information and helps with real-world interaction. She has created a smartphone app called NavCog that talks to users as they walk through buildings, guiding them with directions and letting them know what's nearby. The app makes it much easier for blind people to walk through public places on their own, giving them more independence—which Asakawa has dreamed about since she lost her sight. The app already works in a few locations, such as Carnegie Mellon University, Pittsburgh International Airport, and a few places in Japan.

Asakawa credits all of the groundbreaking technologies she's created to her disability. "Blindness is my strength, not my disadvantage," she says, explaining that losing her sight was the inspiration and motivation behind her drive to invent new technologies. And she thinks anyone who works hard and uses their own challenges to give them strength will succeed. "When you face two options, choose the more challenging one—don't choose the easier option. And finish what you start" is her advice to young people. "You can make the impossible possible by never giving up."

"EVERYBODY HAS DIFFERENT EXPERIENCES, AND YOUR EXPERIENCES MAY HAVE GAPS WITH OTHER PEOPLE IN YOUR WORKPLACE, BUT **THESE GAPS YIELD INNOVATION.**"

Hannah Herbst

FIND **INSPIRATION** IN NATURE

Hannah Herbst is a teenager from Florida who enjoys theater, sports, and hanging out at the beach with her friends. And ever since her father made her to go to a robotics camp the summer before seventh grade, another one of her favorite things to do is to invent things. While observing the world around her, she has come up with clever inventions, including one that earned her the title of "America's Top Young Scientist" for winning a national science fair.

Around the same time that Hannah went to robotics camp at age 12, she learned that her Ethiopian pen pal, Ruth, lived without electricity and dependable drinking water. This problem stuck with Hannah, and she wished there was some way she could help. Then one day, when she was 15, she was fishing off the side of a pier with her family and she "saw this huge boat being completely turned by this current energy in the water," she says. "And I thought it was really interesting, how the water was capable of moving that big boat all on its own." Suddenly, her mind connected the dots between her pen pal's lack of electricity and the energy created by the ocean. She imagined a small device that would collect energy from the ocean's current and store it so it could later be used to supply power for basic necessities like lights.

Excited by her idea, Hannah immediately jumped into action. But before actually trying to build anything, she got permission from the city to conduct experiments with her device in the Boca Raton inlet. She also shot underwater video in the inlet to examine the ocean's environment. Next, she planned out her device, which she called BEACON (Bringing Electricity Access to Countries through Ocean Energy). She began by creating a computer-aided design (CAD) model to avoid major flaws. Then she built it. BEACON was made up of a base with 3-D-printed propellers that the ocean current would spin. The spinning propeller would then start up a *hydroelectric generator* (an engine that converts mechanical power, such as the power created by the spinning propeller, into electricity), which was inside the device.

It wasn't easy, and Hannah had many failed attempts, but she has said that failure is unavoidable for inventors (so get used to it!). Whenever something went wrong, she reminded herself of what light bulb inventor Thomas Edison said: "I have not failed. I've just found 10,000 ways that won't work." Another of her favorite Edison quotations is: "Many of life's failures are people who did not realize how close they were to success when they gave up."

And, lucky for Hannah, it didn't take 10,000 mistakes for her to get BEACON to work! She says that if it were scaled up, her prototype could charge up to three car batteries at the same time in under an hour. She entered it in the 2015 3M Young Scientist Challenge, and a few weeks later, while working on her project, she

FIND INSPIRATION IN THE ANIMAL KINGDOM

Did you know that sharkskin has a special pattern of tiny bumps on it that prevents bacteria from settling on the skin? Hannah knew this, and it inspired another brilliant invention. When her father had surgery that led to a severe infection, Hannah says, "I wanted to find a way that I could prevent these infections from happening again." So she created a reusable, sharkskin-inspired bandage that is made with the same bumpy pattern. Her bandage covers a wound to protect it, but it also "doubles as an antibacterial surface" so that bacteria can't sneak in and cause an infection. In 2019, her bandage won a prize of $5,000 in the Intel International Science and Engineering Fair.

got a phone call from 3M. "I was so excited to be a finalist!" she later said. But she also knew that meant the hard work had just begun. For the next five months, she worked with a mentor that 3M assigned to her and continued to improve her invention. There were many challenges, like figuring out how to protect BEACON from being damaged by saltwater. She also came up with a way to make the device more stationary so that a person doesn't have to uncomfortably bend over and hold it by hand while it's charging in the water.

Before the winners of the 3M contest were announced, Hannah compared herself to the other contestants. "All of their projects were very science-y and programming-oriented, and I'm not that great of a programmer," she later said. "I was a little intimidated by that because my project is not a coding project." But in the end, Hannah won first prize, which included a $25,000 award!

"PROBLEMS CAN'T STOP YOU, OBSTACLES CAN'T STOP YOU, MOST OF ALL OTHER PEOPLE CAN'T STOP YOU—THE ONLY PERSON WHO CAN STOP YOU IS YOURSELF."

Hannah has smart advice for other teens with great ideas: 1) be confident and positive, 2) surround yourself with people who have similar interests, 3) collaborate with others, 4) enter the 3M challenge, and 5) "DON'T GIVE UP!" Coming from an award-winning teenage inventor, these are words to follow.

Temple Grandin

THINKING **DIFFERENTLY** CAN BE A SUPERPOWER

Temple Grandin didn't talk until she was nearly four years old. Instead, she would scream and hum to communicate. When she was diagnosed with autism, a social disability that was misunderstood in the early 1950s, doctors suggested that she live in a hospital. Fortunately, her mother disagreed and raised her at home. When Grandin was in elementary school, she had a white mouse named Crusader. "I was very protective of Crusader and was worried that our cat might eat him," she later said. So she fixed the problem by making his cage safer. "Securing the door with a safety pin made it impossible for our cat to open it."

Decades later, Grandin is still helping animals. She says her autism makes it difficult for her to understand the way other people think and experience emotions. She thinks in pictures, the way animals do. For instance, when she remembers things, she sees the memories in her head, as if she were watching a slideshow. Being a "visual thinker," as she calls it, allows her to observe things that other people might not notice.

For example, when Grandin started working on ranches in Arizona, she often witnessed cows that were terrified by things most people didn't even think about, like things hanging in their path or being steered toward the sun, which stopped them in their tracks.

"If you take a jacket and you put it on a fence, and then you try to drive the cattle by it, they'll be afraid of it. Something that's new is scary when you shove it in their face," she says. "But if I take a jacket and hang it on the side of the fence in a pasture, they'll come up and sniff it. It's attractive if they can voluntarily approach it."

Another thing she noticed was the pathways—or cattle chutes—that ranchers use to herd cattle from one part of the ranch to another were curved in ways that made cows anxious. "The animal, when it starts to walk up the chutes, has to see that there's a place to go. If you bend it too sharply, it does not work," she says. The cows would frequently panic while making their way through the chutes, causing them to have accidents that would often harm or even kill them. Grandin, who lives with anxiety, relates to their panic. And she feels at home with cows in a pasture. "When I'm with cattle," she has said, "I know what the cow's feeling."

So Grandin made it a life mission to change the living conditions of cattle. With a PhD in animal science, she has become famous for redesigning cattle chutes that make cows feel calm. "I looked at specific examples of things that already existed. I took the good bits and threw away the bad bits," she says. She kept the chutes curved, because if they are straight, a cow can see too much going on, which can make them nervous. But she changed the shape of the curves, making them wider and more gradual than the sharply bent ones the ranches had, so the cows could see a few feet ahead and not come across any surprises. She also created the chutes with solid sides,

LEARNING BY PRETENDING

Before Grandin could begin designing better livestock facilities, she first needed to learn how to draw them. At age 28, she had no drafting experience. What she did have was an interesting way of learning. She simply mimicked a designer she knew, David, as he worked. "I went and got exactly the same instruments and pencils as he used . . . and then I started pretending I *was* him," she has said. "The drawing did itself, and, when it was all done, I couldn't believe I'd done it. I didn't have to learn how to draw or design, I pretended I was David—I appropriated him, drawing and all."

rather than with bars that are "see-through," so cows don't get spooked by any commotion going on around them. Finally, she educated ranchers on what can frighten cattle, such as hanging clothes over the chute's walls.

Half of the cattle in the United States and many from around the world now use her chutes and other compassionate innovations. She has made her design plans available online for anyone to use. Grandin's designs are helping to revolutionize the cattle industry, making cows feel calmer and happier, which in turn makes a better, more humane business for the ranchers. She was named one of the "Most Influential People in the World" by *Time* magazine in 2010, and HBO made a movie about her called *Temple Grandin*.

Restricted Space Forcing Pen Plan

"MY APPROACH WAS NOT TO REINVENT THE WHEEL, BUT TO COME UP WITH SOMETHING BETTER."

Grandin, who is also a professor at Colorado State University, says in order to be successful, it's important to try all different kinds of things and to "learn how to do stuff! Find out what you love and find out what you hate." Then, she says, "make yourself really good at something."

Although she was teased in school for being autistic, she now embraces it. Grandin speaks about it publicly and has recently said, "I like the really logical way I think." She says her autism gives her strengths that other people don't have. "I am different, not less." And it's her differences that have allowed her to change an entire industry and invent better living conditions for farm animals around the world.

Rachel Zimmerman Brachman

PUT YOUR SKILLS TO WORK
HELPING OTHERS

In 1982, Rachel Zimmerman Brachman learned how to code. She was only 10 years old, and her single mother, who owned a software company, taught her the basics. Two years later, Brachman used her coding skills to become an award-winning inventor!

Brachman, from Ontario, Canada, was a Girl Guide in elementary school. Her troop had a member who was deaf, so she learned how to *fingerspell* (spelling out words using sign language) in order to communicate with her friend. Brachman then became interested in communication for the disabled. One day, while looking at books about Helen Keller (who was deaf and blind) in the library, Brachman found a book about *Blissymbols*—a type of "alphabet" that uses simple drawings to represent different words. For example, a heart means "feeling," a triangle means "nature," and a circle means "sun." In the 1970s, disabled people who couldn't write or speak—such as those with cerebral palsy—used Blissymbols to communicate by pointing to the drawings on a large board. It was time-consuming and required a person who knew Blissymbols to help translate.

This sparked an idea. What if Brachman programmed a printer to transcribe Blissymbols into text? Disabled people could tap symbols displayed on a touchpad, and the printer would spit out a message for others to read. Brachman set out to make her idea a reality. It wasn't easy. "The hardest part was learning some of the programming skills," she says. Although she had knowledge of the computer program called BASIC, she said, "I definitely had to learn a lot more programming than I already knew going into this." One thing that stumped her was programming the human-to-machine interaction. "If there are 100 symbols on the board, how do you tell the computer which symbol you're pointing at?" But Brachman was determined to finish what she started, taking more coding lessons from her mother as well as from another teacher. "I think a key to becoming a good inventor is not just coming up with the ideas, but then actually making them work," she said.

And her efforts paid off. While she was in the seventh grade, her "Blissymbol printer," which translated symbols into both English and French, won a silver medal at a Canada-wide science fair. She was also invited to exhibit her printer at the World Exhibition of Achievements of Young Inventors in 1985, all the way in Bulgaria.

"ONE OF THE ADVANTAGES THAT AMATEUR INVENTORS HAVE OVER PROFESSIONALS IS THAT THEY DON'T HAVE THE PRECONCEIVED NOTIONS AS TO WHAT SHOULD BE POSSIBLE."

"I was 13, and my parents had to decide whether to let me travel to Bulgaria with a chaperone they had never met before," she says. "And they did. And I went."

Although Brachman had a future as an inventor and engineer, she learned another skill set that would lead her to an out-of-this-world job at NASA. She studied space science at the International Space University (yes, there is such a school!). After getting her master's degree, Brachman ended up working on NASA's Cassini program, the incredible mission to Saturn. She helped educate students about everything NASA learned from their exploration of the faraway planet.

The Cassini mission ended in 2017 after NASA lost contact with the spacecraft, but Brachman still works at NASA's Jet Propulsion Laboratory in Pasadena, California. She also works at an organization called Science Education for Students with Disabilities. Her advice to young STEM students is to keep an open mind about what you want to do after college. "If you told me when I was 12 that I was going to end up working on a mission to Saturn, I would have laughed, because there was no such thing as a mission to Saturn when I was 12," she says. In other words, "The job you end up with may not exist yet, so be flexible."

STUDYING SATURN

NASA sent the Cassini spacecraft to Saturn in 1997 and, in 2004, it was the first probe ever to enter the faraway planet's orbit. While Brachman didn't start working for NASA until 2003, she learned through Cassini's mission that Titan, one of Saturn's moons, has ice volcanoes that spew ice and other materials, creating one of Saturn's rings. She also found out that some of Saturn's rings are spewing out ice and dust that are clumping up into five brand-new tiny moons. The 20-year-long space mission revealed many amazing things about Saturn! And Brachman was able to share her excitement by traveling to schools and teaching young students everything she learned.

Keiana Cavé

ENTER A SCIENCE FAIR TO TAKE YOUR IDEA TO THE **NEXT LEVEL**

When Keiana Cavé moved from Miami to New Orleans in the eighth grade, she noticed a strange smell in the air. She soon realized it was fumes from the Deepwater Horizon oil spill, which had happened a few years earlier, in 2010, in the Gulf of Mexico, about 130 miles away. Deepwater Horizon was the worst environmental disaster in US history. A layer of oil was still floating on the ocean. During the day, the sun shined down on it, but nobody realized how dangerous that was—until Cavé got involved.

Faintly remembering something she had learned about the sun's UV rays, Cavé suspected that the ocean's solar-heated layer of oil was affecting her health. "I knew it was doing something to me, I just didn't know what," she later said. She wondered what officials were doing about it. But when she googled words like "oil spill photochemicals toxic," there were no results. She tried different Google searches, but nothing came up. She was shocked.

She then emailed about 30 professors to tell them she thought the sun hitting the polluted ocean was really dangerous. She did not personally know any of the professors, but she wanted to get their thoughts. Twenty-eight of them responded by laughing it off, as if her idea was overdramatic. Fortunately, two of the experts took her seriously, and one even mentored her for years to come.

By the time Cavé was a sophomore in high school, she was consumed with researching the oil spill herself. She dropped all of her activities (including four sports and two musical instruments), because this was more important to her. Every day after school, she ran across the street to Tulane University to do her research in one of their labs, often staying until after midnight. She needed to prove that UV rays from the sun beating down on the water's surface created new chemicals—chemicals that could cause cancer. And after she proved the existence of the problem, she wanted to fix it.

When she told her mom that she wanted to invent a *molecule* (two or more atoms connected together) that would break apart the oil-spill chemicals and make them nontoxic, her mother, like the professors, laughed at her. Not in a mean way, but in a way that said, "Keep dreaming, kiddo." But Cavé was determined to prove the oil spill had created toxins.

When she was 16, one of her teachers saw what she was working on and encouraged her to enter it in the local science fair. Cavé was astonished when her project won. Her project then moved on to the Earth and environmental sciences category of the 2015 Intel International Science and Engineering Fair, where she competed against 1,700 other students. She didn't think she had a chance. "And then they got to second place, and I heard my named called, and my

"WHETHER YOU REALIZE IT OR NOT, YOU ARE CONSTANTLY MAKING SPLIT-SECOND DECISIONS, AND THESE DECISIONS WILL DETERMINE WHETHER YOU ARE ONE STEP CLOSER OR ONE STEP FARTHER AWAY FROM YOUR GOALS."

jaw dropped," she says. "I had a piece of gum that I was still chewing. It was kind of embarrassing. I was definitely caught off guard."

To make things even more special, because of her high placement in the fair, NASA and MIT Lincoln Laboratory named a minor planet after her. "It's probably one of the most exciting moments still to this day for me," she says.

But the biggest moment came when Chevron, the huge gas corporation, took notice of her. "They saw me speak and reached out and immediately wanted to start funding my project," she says. At age 18, Chevron gave her $1.2 million to further her research! By working with them, Cavé did what no other scientist had done: she invented a molecule that actually neutralizes, or detoxifies, the harmful chemicals in the water. She then created a powder that can be used to spread her molecules over the ocean to make the water safe again.

This is how Cavé became a teenager with two patents. She says that one "is a method they can use right after an oil spill that determines exactly what toxins are in the water," and the other is "a molecule to clean up those toxins." And according to her, Chevron is now working with the Environmental Protection Agency (EPA) to have her molecule used after every oil spill. Cavé's product will have a positive impact all over the world.

Cavé has said that whenever she has one of her big ideas, people laugh at her. But she has learned to welcome the laughter and has said that "maybe it's a good thing to have people laughing, because if your idea is so crazy and so far out of this world, maybe it'll revolutionize an industry."

Inge Lehmann

CHECK YOUR ASSUMPTIONS

Do you know what's at the center of the Earth? A hundred years ago people weren't sure. Science-fiction writers fantasized about prehistoric creatures living deep inside the planet. But most scientists believed it was liquid metal. In reality, it was a mystery. With no ability to see (with our eyes) anything 3,200 miles beneath our feet, how did we ever figure out that Earth's inner core is actually solid? We can thank scientist Inge Lehmann for that.

Born in Copenhagen, Denmark, in 1888, Inge Lehmann lived at a time when it was highly unusual for a woman to be a scientist. But Lehmann was lucky—she went to the first coed high school in Denmark, and they treated girls and boys exactly the same (also highly unusual!). At her school, boys did needlework with the girls, and girls did woodworking, sports, and STEM subjects with the boys. "No difference between the intellect of boys and girls was recognized," Lehmann once wrote. She said it was "a fact that brought some disappointment later in life when I had to recognize that this was not the general attitude."

This type of education allowed Lehmann to shine in math and science, giving her the knowledge and confidence to go for a master's degree in math. But it was *seismology*, the study of earthquakes (which requires lots of math!), that truly fascinated her. "I began to do seismic work and had some extremely interesting years," she once said, referring to a job she took five years after college that sent her to Greenland and other countries to learn about and then install new *seismometers*—devices that measure earthquakes.

During Lehmann's era, scientists already knew that earthquakes were the best "tool" to determine what the inside of our planet is made out of. Earthquakes create energy, called *seismic waves*, that travel through the planet. Back then, scientists noticed that when seismic waves moved through the inside of the planet, they didn't move in a straight line—they would bend. Scientists already knew that seismic waves bend when moving through liquid, so they assumed that Earth's core must be filled with liquid, or *molten rock*— rock so hot that it liquefies. But Lehmann would soon discover that this assumption was wrong.

"YOU SHOULD KNOW HOW MANY **INCOMPETENT** MEN I HAD TO COMPETE WITH—IN VAIN."

After an especially powerful earthquake hit New Zealand in 1929, some of its seismic waves were detected by the newer, more sensitive measuring equipment Lehmann had installed in Scandinavia. This was unexpected, because if Earth's core was liquid as scientists believed, the waves would have bent in the opposite direction, far away from Scandinavia. Something wasn't adding up.

While other scientists blamed it on the seismometers, claiming the devices weren't working properly, Lehmann had a hunch the problem lay somewhere else. She just didn't know where. For years she used her math skills to work on this conundrum, spending hours at a time in her garden calculating numbers. She analyzed all different kinds of seismic data, including the speed, distance, and locations of the waves. She wrote out equations on strips of cardboard that she kept organized in oatmeal boxes. She would spread them all around her, mulling computations over and over in her head.

Then one day, in 1936, it dawned on her: maybe it wasn't the measuring instruments or calculations that were wrong—instead, maybe scientists had the wrong idea about the planet's composition. She redid the math equations, but this time instead of assuming the center of Earth was liquid, she assumed it had a solid core the size of Pluto and a liquid outer core. Suddenly the equations perfectly matched the measurements from the seismometers. It all made sense! Lehmann wrote her hypotheses in a paper called "P," which stands for *P-wave*, the fast-moving type of wave that the European seismometers had detected. ("P" is also the shortest title of any scientific paper ever written.)

While many scientists in history have had a hard time getting others to accept their correct theories, Lehmann was fortunate. Other seismologists read her paper, studied her calculations, and agreed that her conclusion made complete sense—and this validation came at a time when men normally got the credit for women's scientific accomplishments. Bravo, Lehmann!

Lehmann's huge discovery helped scientists better understand the world. And today, scientists are using her same techniques to figure out what makes up the center of Mars. But her career wasn't over yet. She later became an expert on Earth's *upper mantle*, the mostly solid interior section that sits below the planet's outer crust. Lehmann didn't retire until she was in her seventies, and she lived to be 104 years old.

Hadeel Ayoub

TRANSLATE **MOTION** INTO **WORDS**

Hadeel Ayoub loved technology as a kid. Her father taught her how everything in the house worked. She learned to fix their TV, radios, clocks, and even the car. She dreamed of being an engineer, but sadly this was not possible. She lived in Saudi Arabia, a country where women were not encouraged to study technology. So she studied art and design. Never did she imagine that she would invent a high-tech glove to help deaf and nonverbal children communicate.

It wasn't until Ayoub was married with children that she got the opportunity to move out of Saudi Arabia and follow her childhood dream. She studied arts and computational technology in London. "At age 30, I didn't know how to write a single line of code," she says, laughing about how the 20-year-old students had to help her. But what she did know was how to use her engineering skills to tweak a smart glove so she could design things on the computer without using a trackpad. "I didn't want to design using the keyboard. I wanted to draw designs in the air," she says. "The air was my canvas."

Her high-tech glove came in handy when she joined an IBM hackathon, where the goal was to invent something using artificial intelligence to make a positive social change. "Because I already had the tech that understood what my hands were doing in 3-D space, the first thing that came to my mind was sign language," she says. She uses sign language with her young autistic niece.

Ayoub's idea was to reprogram her glove so it could translate the hand positions and movements of sign language into spoken and written language. The text would be spoken aloud through a speaker and displayed on a screen on the wrist part of the glove. This would allow deaf people and people with speech disabilities to easily communicate with those who don't know sign language.

For one month, the glove was all she thought about. "I had this glove fever. I wouldn't sleep. I lost track of time and food, and I was just this zombie working on this," Ayoub says. "But looking back on it, it was a lot of fun." She only meant the glove to be part of an interactive art project, but after publicity from the hackathon, she got hundreds of emails from strangers asking where they could buy the gloves. This got her thinking that maybe it was a product the world could use. She was also motivated by her little niece's reaction to the glove. "The rewarding moment for me was when she figured out that what she was signing was actually being spoken out," Ayoub says. "She just started running in circles because she was so excited. She wouldn't take it off."

Improving her smart glove since 2014, Ayoub launched BrightSign, a company that sells the gloves online. She started with gloves for children, who can choose a design (rainbows, unicorns, pigs, superheroes, etc.). But after a hefty order for the adult employees of a big supermarket chain, she's now making gloves for all ages.

Ayoub says a big challenge for inventors is when people doubt your idea. "Someone will always be around to tell you it can't be done," she says. "But that doesn't translate into 'No, you can't do it.' For me, it actually translates into 'Bring it on.'"

"DON'T THINK THAT BECAUSE IT'S NEVER BEEN DONE, IT MEANS IT CAN'T BE DONE."

Monica Gagliano

DESIGN THE PERFECT EXPERIMENT

When scientist Charles Darwin first discovered *evolution*—the idea that living creatures change over the centuries—the world laughed at him. In the 1800s, people thought animals and humans were all created simultaneously without evolving. It took decades for Darwin's ideas to be accepted. Today, scientist Monica Gagliano faces a similar challenge with her experiments that suggest that plants have memories and can even be trained—like dogs.

Born in Italy, Gagliano is a marine biologist who experiments on plants the same way she would on animals. One of her famous studies was based on the 20th-century "Pavlov's dog" experiments, in which scientist Ivan Pavlov rang a bell whenever his dog was about to be fed. When the dog saw the food, it drooled. Finally, Pavlov rang the bell without serving food, but the dog still salivated, teaching us that the dog *remembered* and associated the bell with the food.

At the University of Western Australia, Gagliano conducted a similar experiment on plants called the Pavlovian Pea. But instead of a bell, she used a fan, which she says "doesn't mean anything to the plant." Instead of dog food, she used a blue light, which was like "dinner for the plant," since plants grow toward blue light. For the experiment, she grew pea plants in Y-shaped planters and put them in a dark room. For one group of planters, she aimed a blue light and

fan at the plants from the same branch of the Y. For the second group, the light and fan faced the plants from opposite sides of the Y. (She also had a control group of plants without a light or fan.) After three days, she turned off the blue lights and moved each fan to the other side of the plants. She wondered if the plants that had started with the light and fan together would bend toward the new location of the fan, even though the blowing air wasn't accompanied by light.

At first, "it looked like it wasn't working," says Gagliano. The plants were not changing directions. "I thought, 'I'm just going to give up. I tried, but the plants probably cannot learn this way.'" But then, "I was about to turn everything off, and I just peeked one more time at my plants, and suddenly I realized they were showing me exactly what I was hoping they would do!" The plants that started with the fan and light on the same side started bending the *other way* to face the fan's new location, without the blue light. The other plants, that hadn't been "trained" to associate the fan with the light, did not react to the fan—they kept facing the light, which, again, wasn't even on.

Many scientists admit that her experiment was done correctly but doubt her conclusion that plants have memories. "Their reactions were quite aggressive," she says. But she doesn't let criticism stop her. After publishing her work in science journals, she says the science community at least believes her experiments work. How to interpret them—Do plants think? Or are they reacting mechanically?—is still up for debate. Without answers, she says it is "unscientific" *not* to continue with experiments. "If we don't have an answer, the question is valid and we should chase it."

> **"TO ME, THE ROLE OF A SCIENTIST IS TO EXPLORE— AND TO EXPLORE ESPECIALLY WHAT WE DON'T KNOW."**

Ayah Bdeir

INVENT THE WORLD YOU WANT TO LIVE IN

Ayah Bdeir admits that she was "that kid." You know, the hyper one with good grades who challenges everything the teacher says. The adventurous one who gets time-outs for not listening to the word "no." The curious one who upsets her friends by breaking open their toys to see what's inside. Bdeir says being "that kid" got her labeled as a "troublemaker," but it's also what led her to take risks and become the founder of littleBits, a multimillion-dollar company that makes electronics kits for kids.

Growing up in Lebanon, Bdeir always had an interest in making things, and her parents "never let [her] gender come into play" when buying her toys. They got her electricity sets, chemistry kits, Lego bricks, video games, and lessons in how to create software. She loved taking things apart to see how they worked. "My sisters learned quickly not to leave their toys with me," she says. "It was also a bad idea to leave electronic devices near me—I dismantled the VCR once and got into a lot of trouble!"

Bdeir says she never wanted to be an engineer, which sounded "pretty dry and boring," until she moved to the United States and went to graduate school at the MIT Media Lab. That's where she realized "you could combine engineering with art and design and prototyping tools to create really amazing things!" She fantasized about inventing magnetic electronics kits that would be "like candy" to kids and that would make engineering fun, even for non-experts.

But this great idea came to a halt after MIT when she took a job as a software consultant. This was considered a "good job," but she wasn't happy. There was nothing for her to build, and nothing for her to take apart! She missed experimenting and wondered if other creative people felt trapped in careers that didn't let them be themselves. And then she made a decision: if she wanted a different life, she would have to be "that kid" and invent it.

So Bdeir took a risk and quit her job. Her plan was to create a kit of candy-colored electronic pieces, or "bits." Each color would have a different function. For instance, blue bits would power up your creation, while green bits would be output pieces that would allow you to add things like motors, horns, buzzers, and lights. Users could mix and match the bits to make anything from musical instruments and interactive games to robots and light-up accessories.

At first, creating her kits was really hard, and her confidence started to wobble. Her first prototype took two months to make, and the pieces kept conking out on her. But she was eager to see how people would react, so she gathered her courage and brought her handmade bits to the the 2009 Maker Faire in San Mateo, California. Standing behind her booth, she was embarrassed that her

SWAP GREAT IDEAS ONLINE

What sets littleBits apart from other companies is its online "club" that anyone can join. Check out their open source library, where thousands of makers have shared littleBits instructions for their own projects. In the beginning, sometimes when a project got more than 1,000 votes, littleBits would sell the invention and pay the creator a percentage of the profits!

And then there's YouTube. When Bdeir visited the site, she was stunned to see all the amazing things people had made: a "thief detector" that texts you if someone breaks into your stuff, a light-up skirt, glow-in-the-dark headbands, a snack-serving robot, a vending machine that attaches to your backpack . . . and the list goes on. LittleBits is more than a company—it's a community.

demonstrations kept failing. She and her team had to keep jiggling the parts to get them to work. She worried that people would think she was a "fraud." But then something amazing happened.

Even though the kits back then weren't meant for children, "lines and lines of kids were forming, and they were snapping things together, asking questions, laughing, playing, showing each other things, showing their parents things," she recalls. "And I thought, 'Wow! Kids are really taking to this!'" They were coming up with all sorts of original—and silly—creations, including buzzing toys, a "penguin finder" (like a metal detector except it finds penguins), and even a "fart sensor." She realized that many children were interested in electronics, but there weren't any fun electronics-for-beginners kits out there to engage them. So she decided to focus on kids and call her product "littleBits."

"WE SPEND 11 HOURS A DAY WITH TECHNOLOGY, AND YET MOST OF US DON'T KNOW HOW IT WORKS OR HOW TO MAKE IT OUR OWN."

She officially launched littleBits in 2011, and it took off. Investors gave Bdeir millions and millions of dollars to build her company, and after around 30 prototypes (yes, 30 different versions of littleBits!), the kits became so popular that even Bdeir was surprised.

Bdeir, who sold littleBits to the high-tech toy company Sphero in 2019, encourages girls and boys to not only be risk-takers who invent things to change the world, but to also invent their own futures. "You are not only a participant in your life—you are your own change-maker," she says. "Learn, have fun, surround yourself with people that share your passions, and invent the world you want to live in!"

LEARN MORE!

BOOKS

101 Great Science Experiments: A Step-by-Step Guide by Neil Ardley (DK Children, 2014).

Awesome Achievers in Science by Alan Katz, illustrated by Chris Judge (Running Press Kids, 2019).

Awesome Achievers in Technology by Alan Katz, illustrated by Chris Judge (Running Press Kids, 2019).

The Girl Who Drew Butterflies: How Maria Merian's Art Changed Science by Joyce Sidman (Houghton Mifflin Harcourt, 2018).

Girls Think of Everything: Stories of Ingenious Inventions by Women by Catherine Thimmesh, illustrated by Melissa Sweet (HMH Books for Young Readers, 2018).

Girls Who Code: Learn to Code and Change the World by Reshma Saujani (Viking Books for Young Readers, 2017).

Headstrong: 52 Women Who Changed Science—and the World by Rachel Swaby (Broadway Books, 2015).

Hidden Figures Young Readers' Edition by Margot Lee Shetterly (Harper, 2016).

Maker Lab: 28 Super Cool Projects by Jack Challoner (DK Children, 2016).

Reaching for the Moon: The Autobiography of NASA Mathematician Katherine Johnson by Katherine Johnson (Atheneum Books for Young Readers, 2019).

Women in Science: 50 Fearless Pioneers Who Changed the World by Rachel Ignotofsky (Ten Speed Press, 2016).

WEBSITES

appinventor.mit.edu
carnegiestemgirls.org
makezine.com/projects

YOUTUBE

BrainCraft
Dr. Becky
GoldieBlox Scrappy Robots
Gross Science
It's Okay to Be Smart
Physics Girl
Tech-nic-Allie Speaking
The Brain Scoop

TED TALKS

Look for TED and TEDx Talks by:

- Chieko Asakawa
- Ayah Bdeir
- Keiana Cavé
- Jane ní Dhulchaointigh
- Pauline van Dongen
- Simone Giertz
- Temple Grandin
- Michelle Oblak
- Sarah Parcak
- Gitanjali Rao
- Carol Reiley
- Martine Rothblatt
- Star Simpson
- Anna Stork and Andrea Sreshta
- Doris Sung
- Fiona Wood

Generation Girl books celebrate amazing women who've been there, done that, and learned some valuable lessons along the way. Be inspired by their stories, learn from their struggles and successes, and get ready to change the world. Look for more hard-won wisdom in: